Knit a square & make a toy

Norma Campbell

The Australian Women's Weekly craft library

Contents

Introduction

Believe it or not, the toys shown on the following pages are all made from garter-stitch squares and rectangles. All the shaping is done at the making-up stage, when the knitted pieces are simply folded under and joined to create the shapes required. As the knitted pieces are not shaped, there are no knitting patterns to follow, so it's almost impossible to make a mistake. That's the beauty of this method — any 'mistakes' made when joining the pieces will contribute to the unique character of the finished toy.

Basic Instructions

MATERIALS

Our toys are made from acrylic 8-ply yarn, but you can substitute wool if you like. If you use a thicker or thinner yarn, though, the toy will be a different size from the one shown. Remember also that if you use a normal yarn when we've specified bouclé, the toy will be smaller, as the bouclé is very stretchy. We've suggested colours according to those shown in the photographed toy, but the colour choice is up to you. Any oddments will do for the embroidery.

For most of the toys, we have used 4mm knitting needles. You will also need a knitter's needle for sewing seams and embroidery. When joining the pieces, use large plastic- or glass-headed pins to prevent the pins being lost in the knitting. Use a white, washable, acrylic toy filling, such as fibrefill, for stuffing.

KNITTING

If you have never knitted before, refer to the Knitting Instructions on page 94. The only abbreviation used in the knitting instructions for the individual toys is st(s) for stitch(es).

On the first page of instructions for each toy there are diagrams of the squares and rectangles — the 'pattern pieces' — required. Using garter stitch (all plain rows, no purl) and yarn of choice, cast on the specified number of stitches for each pattern piece, then knit as many rows as required to make the square or rectangle. (The number of rows given down the side of each square or

rectangle is only a guide.) Make sure the sides of the square are equal and, unless otherwise specified, the long sides of each rectangle are twice the length of the short sides. To create a firm sewing edge, knit into the back of the first stitch in each row. Cast on and off fairly loosely, as squares need to stretch a little when they are stuffed.

Knit all the pieces required for each toy before making up.

MAKING UP

Follow the step-by-step diagrams and refer to the photographs of the finished toy when joining, and shaping, the pieces. Work from the outside — that is, with the wrong sides of the knitted pieces together — and pin the pieces first, making sure the rows run in the same direction as in the photographed toy. Make the shapes shown in the diagrams by folding and then pinning any excess to the inside; the excess becomes part of the stuffing. When you are satisfied with the shape, oversew along the seams indicated on the diagrams, matching the colour of the yarn to your knitting. To allow for the fact that the knitted fabric will stretch when stuffed, stretch the knitting a little when sewing together all pieces except head pieces.

Stuff the toys as you sew, following the instructions. Stuff firmly, but don't overstuff, to avoid stretching the knitting out of shape.

All the toys are child-friendly, so the facial features are embroidered rather than attached. The section on Embroidery Stitches on page 96 clearly illustrates the simple stitches used.

MEASUREMENTS

Approximately 44cm tall.

MATERIALS

8-ply acrylic yarn (50g):

- Two balls yellow
- Small amounts blue and white
- Small amounts dark brown and black, for embroidery
- One pair 4mm (No 8) knitting needles
- Knitter's needle, for sewing seams and embroidery
- Polyester filling
- Ribbon

KNITTING

Note: *Before beginning, it is important to read the **Basic Instructions** on page 5.*

Approximately 48 rows

HEAD
make 2

LEG
make 2

28 stitches

Using yellow, cast on 28 sts.
Knit 48 rows, cast off.

BODY
make 2

ARM
make 2

28 stitches

Using blue, cast on 28 sts. Knit 22 rows in stripes of 2 rows blue and 2 rows white, ending with a blue row. Change to yellow, knit 26 rows, cast off.

Approximately 24 rows

MUZZLE
make 1

28 stitches

Using yellow, cast on 28 sts.
Knit 24 rows, cast off.

TO MAKE UP

1 Matching stripes, join Body squares together along three sides, leaving neck and shoulder edge open.

2 Fold each Arm in half, matching stripes, and join along cast-on edge and long side.

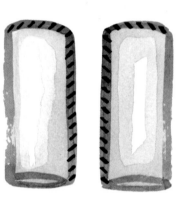

3 Fold each Leg in half, and join along cast-on edge and long side.

4 Join closed ends of Arms and Legs to Body. Stuff Arms and Legs with polyester filling and sew open ends closed, rounding corners. Stuff Body.

Teddy

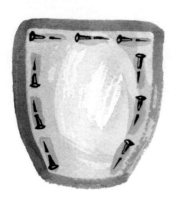

5 Pin Head squares together, rounding top corners and shaping neck.

11 Position Muzzle on lower half of face and sew in place.

6 Sew around edge, leaving neck edge open for stuffing.

8 Insert neck in centre of Body opening, pin then sew neck to neck edge of Body. Add more filling to Body, if necessary, and sew shoulder seams.

9 Fold Muzzle in half widthwise, sew lower seam and run a gathering thread around one open end.

12 Using dark brown, work eyes in satin stitch and mouth in stem stitch. Using black, work nose in satin stitch. Tie a ribbon around Teddy's neck to finish.

7 Sew diagonally across top corners of Head to form ears. Run a gathering thread around neck edge and top of neck. Stuff Head, pull up neck gathering to approximately 19cm, and stuff neck.

10 Pull up gathering tightly and tie off. Stuff Muzzle firmly.

Cat

MEASUREMENTS

Approximately 44cm tall.

MATERIALS

8-ply acrylic yarn (50g):

- ■ Two balls orange
- ■ Small amounts white and black
- ■ Small amounts green and dark brown, for embroidery
- ■ One pair 4mm (No 8) knitting needles
- ■ Knitter's needle, for sewing seams and embroidery
- ■ Polyester filling
- ■ Ribbon

KNITTING

Note: *Before beginning, it is important to read the Basic Instructions on page 5.*

Approximately 48 rows

HEAD
make 2

BODY
make 2

28 stitches

Using orange, cast on 28 sts. Knit 48 rows, cast off.

Approximately 48 rows

ARM
make 2

LEG
make 2

28 stitches

Using orange, cast on 28 sts. Knit 44 rows. Change to black, knit 4 rows, cast off.

Approximately 24 rows

MUZZLE
make 1

14 stitches

Using white, cast on 14 sts, Knit 24 rows, cast off.

Approximately 72 rows

TAIL
make 1

14 stitches

Using orange, cast on 14 sts. Knit 72 rows in random stripe pattern, alternating orange and white, cast off.

TO MAKE UP

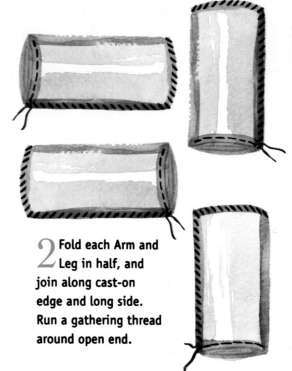

2 Fold each Arm and Leg in half, and join along cast-on edge and long side. Run a gathering thread around open end.

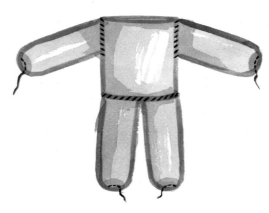

3 Join closed ends of Arms and Legs to Body. Stuff Arms and Legs with polyester filling, pull up gathering tightly and tie off. Stuff Body.

1 Join Body squares together along three sides, leaving neck and shoulder edge open.

4 Pin Head squares together, folding in lower corners to shape neck.

5 Sew around edge, leaving neck edge open for stuffing.

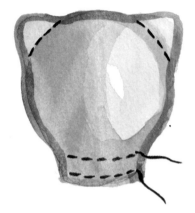

6 Sew diagonally across top corners of Head to form ears. Run a gathering thread around neck edge and top of neck. Stuff Head, pull up neck gathering to approximately 20cm, and stuff neck.

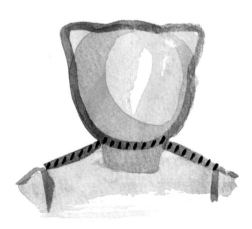

7 Insert neck in centre of Body opening, pin then sew neck to neck edge of Body. Add more filling to Body, if necessary, and sew shoulder seams.

8 Fold Tail in half lengthwise and sew long seam, folding in one end to create a point. Stuff well, sew open end closed, and join to lower back Body.

9 Run a heart-shaped row of gathering stitches around centre of Muzzle.

10 Pull up gathering and pin Muzzle onto face, folding edges under to create elongated heart shape shown. Sew in place, adding a little polyester filling, if necessary.

11 Using black and green, work eyes in satin stitch. Using black, work nose in satin stitch and whiskers in straight stitch. Using dark brown, work mouth in stem stitch. Tie a ribbon around Cat's neck to finish.

MEASUREMENTS

Approximately 18cm long x 20cm high.

MATERIALS

8-ply acrylic yarn (50g):

- Two balls yellow
- Small amount orange
- Small amount black, for embroidery
- One pair 4mm (No 8) knitting needles
- One pair 2.75mm (No 12) knitting needles
- Knitter's needle, for sewing seams and embroidery
- Polyester filling
- Ribbon

KNITTING

Note: *Before beginning, it is important to read the* **Basic Instructions** *on page 5.*

Approximately 24 rows

WING
make 2

FOOT
make 2

14 stitches *14 stitches*

Using 4mm needles and yellow for Wings and orange for Feet, cast on 14 sts. Knit 24 rows, cast off.

Approximately 48 rows

BODY
make 2

28 stitches

Using 4mm needles and yellow, cast on 28 sts. Knit 48 rows, cast off.

Approximately 24 rows

HEAD
make 1

28 stitches

Using 4mm needles and yellow, cast on 28 sts. Knit 24 rows, cast off.

Approximately 12 rows

TAIL
make 1

7 stitches

Using 4mm needles and yellow, cast on 7 sts. Knit 12 rows, cast off.

Approximately 24 rows

BILL
make 2

14 stitches

Using 2.75mm needles and orange, cast on 14 sts. Knit 24 rows in stocking stitch (see page 95), cast off.

TO MAKE UP

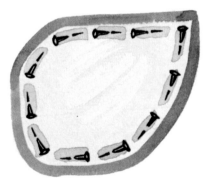

1 Pin Body squares together, folding edges under to create shape shown.

2 Sew around Body, leaving a 6cm neck opening in top seam. Stuff with polyester filling.

3 Fold Head in half widthwise to find centre and mark with pin. Matching pin with top Body seam, join one long side of Head to neck opening.

Duck

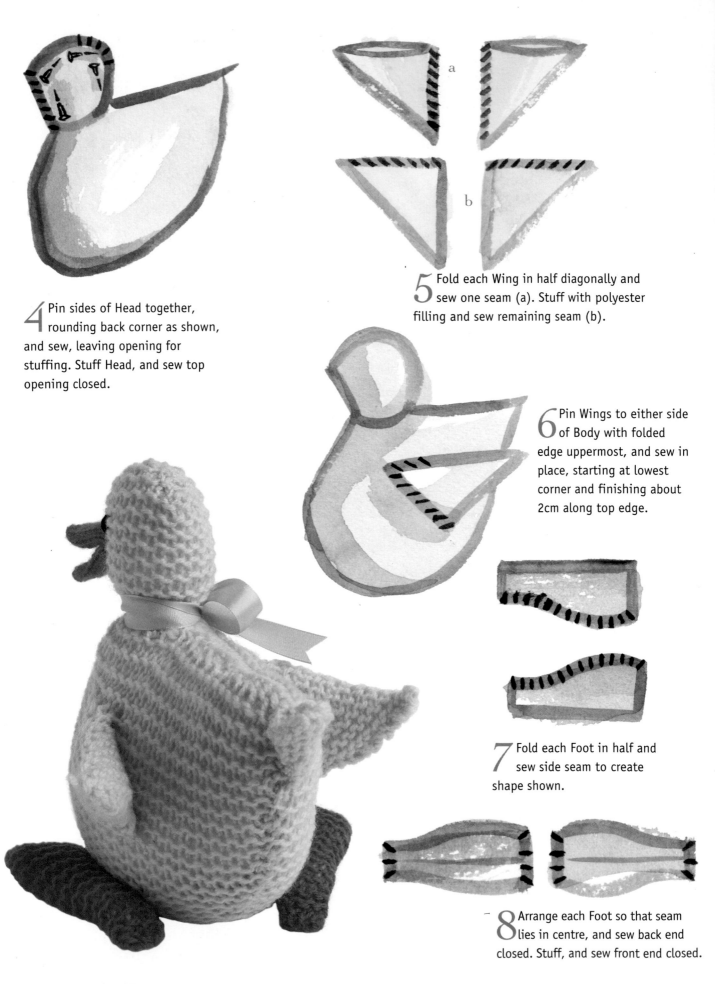

4 Pin sides of Head together, rounding back corner as shown, and sew, leaving opening for stuffing. Stuff Head, and sew top opening closed.

a

b

5 Fold each Wing in half diagonally and sew one seam (a). Stuff with polyester filling and sew remaining seam (b).

6 Pin Wings to either side of Body with folded edge uppermost, and sew in place, starting at lowest corner and finishing about 2cm along top edge.

7 Fold each Foot in half and sew side seam to create shape shown.

8 Arrange each Foot so that seam lies in centre, and sew back end closed. Stuff, and sew front end closed.

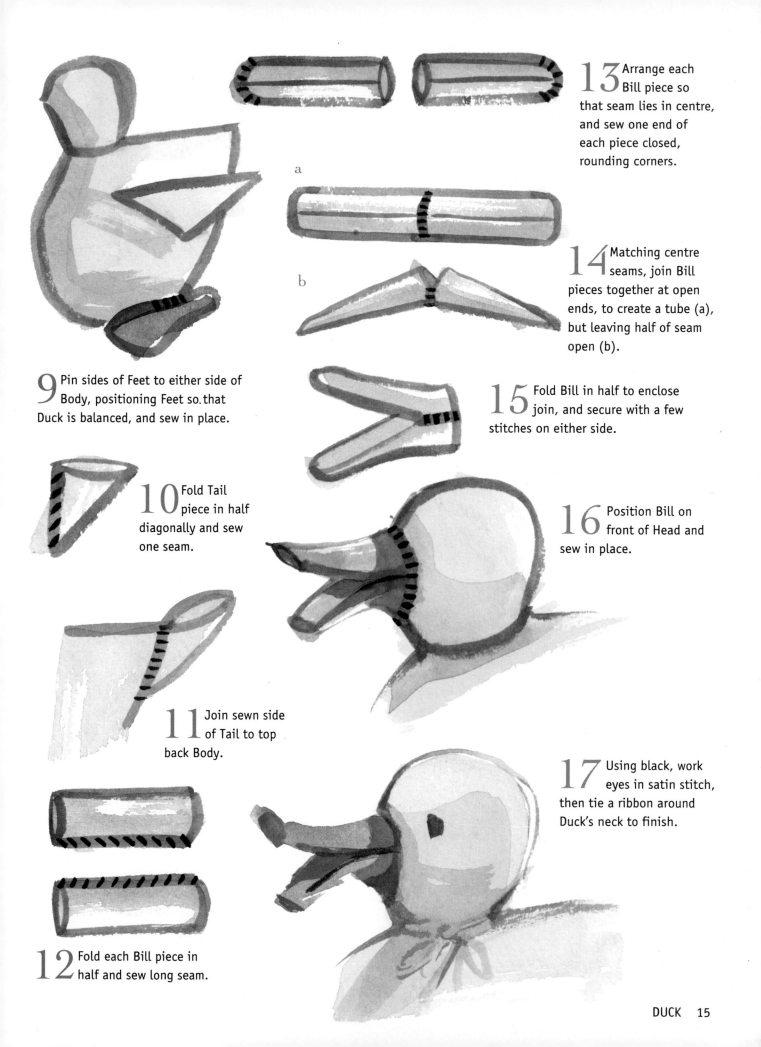

13 Arrange each Bill piece so that seam lies in centre, and sew one end of each piece closed, rounding corners.

a

b

14 Matching centre seams, join Bill pieces together at open ends, to create a tube (a), but leaving half of seam open (b).

9 Pin sides of Feet to either side of Body, positioning Feet so that Duck is balanced, and sew in place.

15 Fold Bill in half to enclose join, and secure with a few stitches on either side.

10 Fold Tail piece in half diagonally and sew one seam.

16 Position Bill on front of Head and sew in place.

11 Join sewn side of Tail to top back Body.

17 Using black, work eyes in satin stitch, then tie a ribbon around Duck's neck to finish.

12 Fold each Bill piece in half and sew long seam.

MEASUREMENTS

Approximately 34cm high (including ears).

MATERIALS

8-ply acrylic yarn (50g):

■ Two balls blue (or colour of choice)
■ Small amounts black and red, for embroidery
■ One pair 4mm (No 8) knitting needles
■ Knitter's needle, for sewing seams and embroidery
■ Polyester filling

KNITTING

Note: *Before beginning, it is important to read the **Basic Instructions** on page 5.*

Approximately 48 rows

LOWER BACK BODY
make 2

HIP
make 2

28 stitches

Using blue, cast on 28 sts. Knit 48 rows, cast off.

Approximately 24 rows

LEG
make 2

TAIL
make 1

28 stitches

Using blue, cast on 28 sts. Knit 24 rows, cast off.

Approximately 48 rows

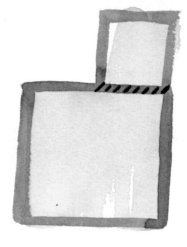

LOWER FRONT BODY
make 1

14 stitches

Using blue, cast on 14 sts. Knit 48 rows, cast off.

Approximately 24 rows

make 9
SEE BELOW

14 stitches

Using blue, cast on 14 sts. Knit 24 rows, cast off.

TOP BACK BODY
make 2

TOP FRONT BODY
make 1

HEAD
make 1

ARM
make 2

EAR
make 2

POUCH
make 1

TO MAKE UP

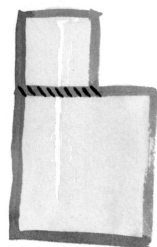

1 Join each Top Back Body to a Lower Back Body, to form two back pieces.

2 Join Top Front Body to Lower Front Body, to form front piece.

3 Join a back piece to each side of front piece, adjusting so that top inner corners of back pieces almost meet at centre front, to form body piece.

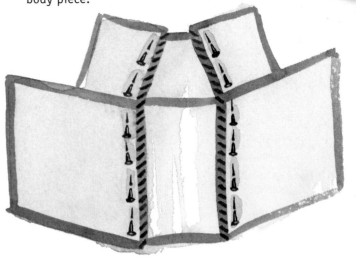

Kangaroo

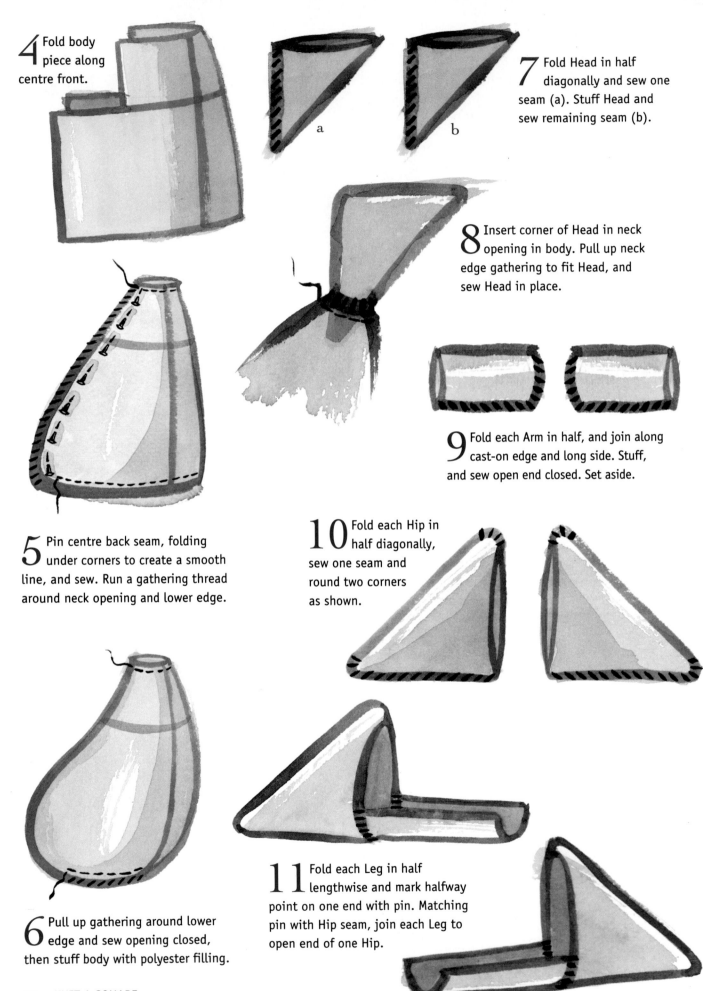

4 Fold body piece along centre front.

5 Pin centre back seam, folding under corners to create a smooth line, and sew. Run a gathering thread around neck opening and lower edge.

6 Pull up gathering around lower edge and sew opening closed, then stuff body with polyester filling.

7 Fold Head in half diagonally and sew one seam (a). Stuff Head and sew remaining seam (b).

a

b

8 Insert corner of Head in neck opening in body. Pull up neck edge gathering to fit Head, and sew Head in place.

9 Fold each Arm in half, and join along cast-on edge and long side. Stuff, and sew open end closed. Set aside.

10 Fold each Hip in half diagonally, sew one seam and round two corners as shown.

11 Fold each Leg in half lengthwise and mark halfway point on one end with pin. Matching pin with Hip seam, join each Leg to open end of one Hip.

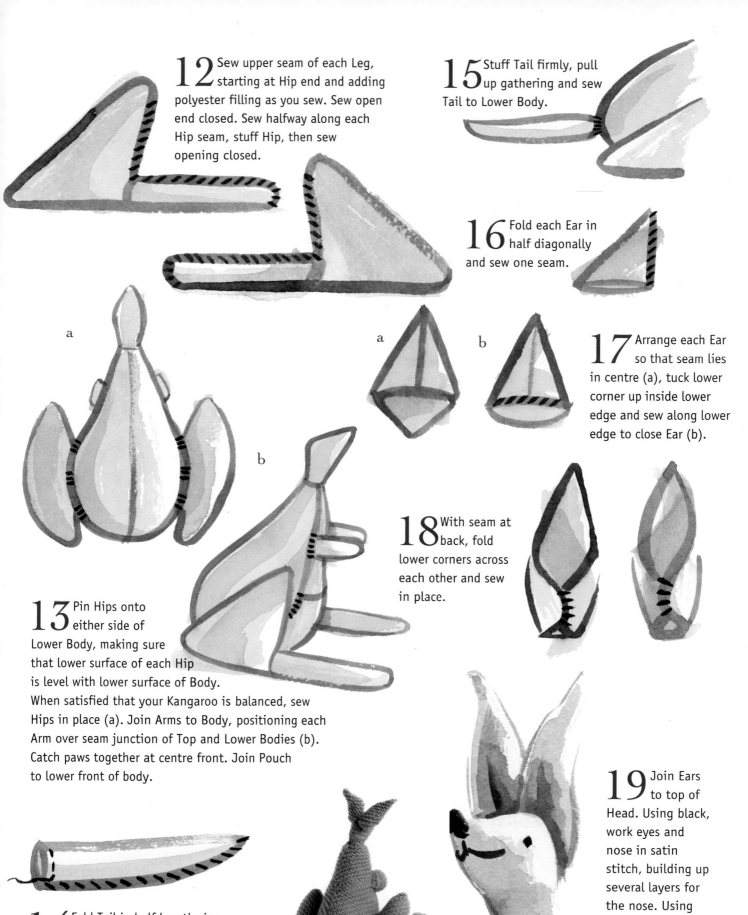

12 Sew upper seam of each Leg, starting at Hip end and adding polyester filling as you sew. Sew open end closed. Sew halfway along each Hip seam, stuff Hip, then sew opening closed.

15 Stuff Tail firmly, pull up gathering and sew Tail to Lower Body.

16 Fold each Ear in half diagonally and sew one seam.

a

b

17 Arrange each Ear so that seam lies in centre (a), tuck lower corner up inside lower edge and sew along lower edge to close Ear (b).

a

b

18 With seam at back, fold lower corners across each other and sew in place.

13 Pin Hips onto either side of Lower Body, making sure that lower surface of each Hip is level with lower surface of Body. When satisfied that your Kangaroo is balanced, sew Hips in place (a). Join Arms to Body, positioning each Arm over seam junction of Top and Lower Bodies (b). Catch paws together at centre front. Join Pouch to lower front of body.

14 Fold Tail in half lengthwise and sew long seam, folding in one end to create a point. Run a gathering thread around open end.

19 Join Ears to top of Head. Using black, work eyes and nose in satin stitch, building up several layers for the nose. Using red, work mouth in straight stitch.

MEASUREMENTS

Approximately 48cm tall.

MATERIALS

8-ply acrylic yarn (50g):

- One ball cream
- Two balls pink
- Small amounts black, yellow and white
- Small amounts dark brown, pink and deep red, for embroidery
- One pair 4mm (No 8) knitting needles
- Knitter's needle, for sewing seams and embroidery
- Crochet hook, for ponytail and fringe
- Polyester filling

KNITTING

Note: *Before beginning, it is important to read the* **Basic Instructions** *on page 5.*

Approximately 48 rows

HEAD
make 2

28 stitches

Using cream, cast on 28 sts.
Knit 48 rows, cast off.

Approximately 48 rows

BODY
make 2

28 stitches

Using pink, cast on 28 sts.
Knit 36 rows, change to white,
knit 2 rows. Change to pink,
knit 10 rows, cast off.

Approximately 24 rows

SKIRT
make 2

52 stitches

Using pink, cast on 52 sts. Knit 18 rows,
change to white, knit 2 rows. Change to pink,
knit 4 rows, cast off.

Approximately 48 rows

HAIR
make 1

14 stitches

Using yellow, cast on 14
sts. Knit 48 rows, cast off.

Approximately 48 rows

ARM
make 2

28 stitches

Using pink, cast on 28 sts.
Knit 26 rows, change to white,
knit 2 rows. Change to pink,
knit 10 rows. Change to cream,
knit 10 rows, cast off.

Approximately 48 rows

LEG
make 2

28 stitches

Using cream, cast on 28 sts.
Knit 42 rows. Change to black,
knit 6 rows, cast off.

TO MAKE UP

1 Matching white stripes, join Body squares together along three sides, leaving neck and shoulder edge open.

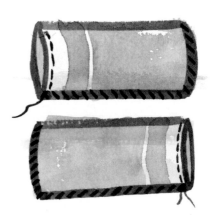

2 Fold each Arm in half, matching stripes, and join along cast-on edge and long side. Run a gathering thread around open end.

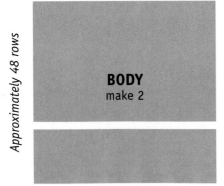

Doll

3 Fold each Leg in half, and join along cast-on edge and long side. Run a gathering thread around open end.

6 Sew around edge, leaving neck edge open for stuffing.

8 Insert neck in centre of Body opening, pin then sew neck to neck edge of Body. Add more filling to Body, if necessary, and sew shoulder seams.

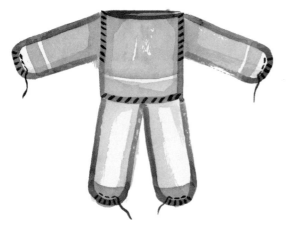

4 Join closed ends of Arms and Legs to Body. Stuff Arms and Legs with polyester filling, pull up gathering and sew open ends closed. Stuff Body.

7 Run a gathering thread around neck edge and top of neck. Stuff Head, pull up neck gathering to approximately 19cm, and stuff neck.

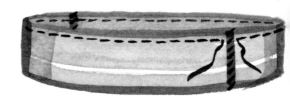

9 Matching stripes, join Skirts together along short ends to form a ring. Run a gathering thread around upper edge.

5 Pin Head squares together, rounding corners and shaping neck.

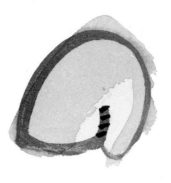

10 Position Skirt about 3cm up from end of Body (just below stripe), pull up gathering to fit Body, placing seams at sides, and sew in place.

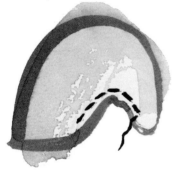

11 Run a gathering thread along one long edge of Hair piece, pull up tightly and tie off.

12 Bring corners of gathered edge together as shown, and sew adjacent sides together; this shapes the Hair piece.

13 Position Hair piece on Head with seam at centre back, and sew in place.

14 To make one ponytail, cut 15 lengths of yellow yarn, each approximately 40cm. Form one or two lengths into a loop and, using crochet hook, pull loop through corner of Hair at side of Head (a). Thread ends through loop and pull to tighten knot (b). Repeat for remaining lengths. Make other ponytail in same way. Use the same method to knot single strands of yellow yarn to make the fringe.

15 Using dark brown for eyes and pink for nose, work features in satin stitch. Using deep red, work mouth in stem stitch. Take a stitch from side to side on each Leg to create knee dimples, and tie a yarn "shoelace" to the front of each shoe.

MEASUREMENTS

Approximately 30cm high.

MATERIALS

8-ply acrylic yarn (50g):

- One ball each black and white
- Small amount yellow
- Small amount aqua, for embroidery
- One pair 4mm (No 8) knitting needles
- Knitter's needle, for sewing seams and embroidery
- Polyester filling

KNITTING

Note: *Before beginning, it is important to read the* **Basic Instructions** *on page 5.*

FLIPPER
make 2

Approximately 48 rows

14 stitches

Using black, cast on 14 sts. Knit 24 rows. Change to white, knit 24 rows, cast off.

BEAK
make 1

Approximately 24 rows

14 stitches

Using black, cast on 14 sts. Knit 24 rows, cast off.

TOP BACK BODY/HEAD
make 2

TAIL
make 1

Approximately 48 rows

14 stitches

TOP FRONT BODY
make 1

14 stitches

FOOT
make 2

14 stitches

Using black for Top Back Body/Head and Tail, white for Top Front Body and yellow for Feet, cast on 14 sts. Knit 48 rows, cast off.

LOWER BACK BODY
make 2

Approximately 48 rows

28 stitches

LOWER FRONT BODY
make 1

28 stitches

Using black for Lower Back Body and white for Lower Front Body, cast on 28 sts. Knit 48 rows, cast off.

TO MAKE UP

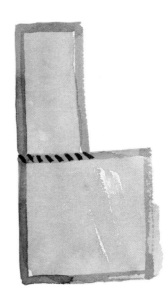
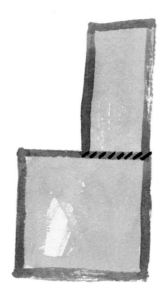

1 Join each Top Back Body/Head to a Lower Back Body, to form two side/back pieces.

2 Join Top Front Body to Lower Front Body, to form front piece.

Penguin

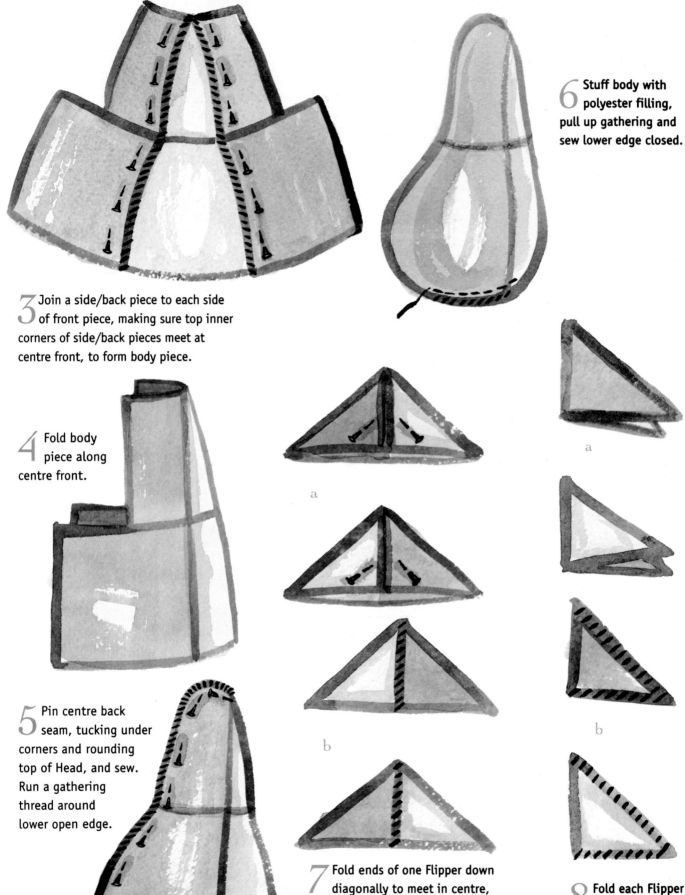

3 Join a side/back piece to each side of front piece, making sure top inner corners of side/back pieces meet at centre front, to form body piece.

4 Fold body piece along centre front.

5 Pin centre back seam, tucking under corners and rounding top of Head, and sew. Run a gathering thread around lower open edge.

6 Stuff body with polyester filling, pull up gathering and sew lower edge closed.

a

b

a

b

7 Fold ends of one Flipper down diagonally to meet in centre, and pin. Repeat for other Flipper, reversing position of black and white (a). Sew seams (b).

8 Fold each Flipper in half, enclosing seam (a), and sew along two sides (b).

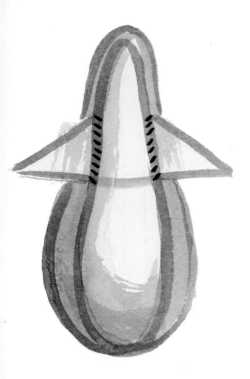

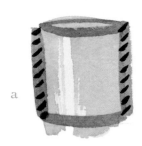

9 Sew a Flipper to each side seam, positioning lower edge of Flipper on horizontal body seam. Make sure black side of each Flipper faces outwards.

11 Fold Tail in half widthwise and sew side seams (a), stuff and sew open end closed (b).

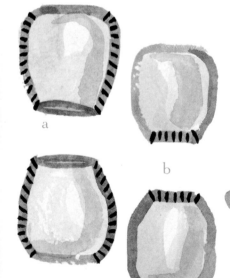

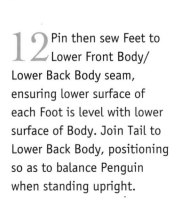

13 Fold Beak in half diagonally and sew one seam. Stuff well.

10 Fold each Foot in half widthwise and sew side seams, rounding corners and tapering Foot slightly towards open end (a). Stuff Foot and sew open end closed (b).

12 Pin then sew Feet to Lower Front Body/ Lower Back Body seam, ensuring lower surface of each Foot is level with lower surface of Body. Join Tail to Lower Back Body, positioning so as to balance Penguin when standing upright.

14 Join open end of Beak to front of Head. Using aqua, work eyes in satin stitch.

MEASUREMENTS

Approximately 40cm high.

MATERIALS

8-ply acrylic yarn (50g):

- Two balls blue
- Small amount brown
- Small amounts various colours, for nose band and neck band
- Small amount black, for embroidery
- One pair 4mm (No 8) knitting needles
- Knitter's needle, for sewing seams and embroidery
- Polyester filling

KNITTING

Note: *Before beginning, it is important to read the **Basic Instructions** on page 5.*

Approximately 48 rows

BODY
make 2

LEG
make 4

NECK
make 1

HEAD
make 1

28 stitches

Using blue, cast on 28 sts. Knit 48 rows, cast off.

Approximately 24 rows

HUMP
make 1

14 stitches

Using blue, cast on 14 sts. Knit 24 rows, cast off.

Approximately 12 rows

KNEE
make 4

7 stitches

Using brown, cast on 7 sts. Knit 12 rows, cast off.

Approximately 6 rows

EAR make 2

14 stitches

Using blue, cast on 14 sts. Knit 6 rows, cast off.

TO MAKE UP

1 Join Body squares together along cast-on and cast-off edges, and run a gathering thread around open ends.

2 Pull up gathering to shape Body, and sew one end closed. Stuff Body with polyester filling, and sew remaining end closed.

3 Fold each Leg in half and sew side seam. Run a gathering thread around open ends.

4 Pull up gathering around one end of each Leg and tie off. Stuff Legs. Pull up gathering slightly around remaining open end of each Leg.

5 Join open ends of Legs to Body, positioning two Legs either side of lower seam.

Camel

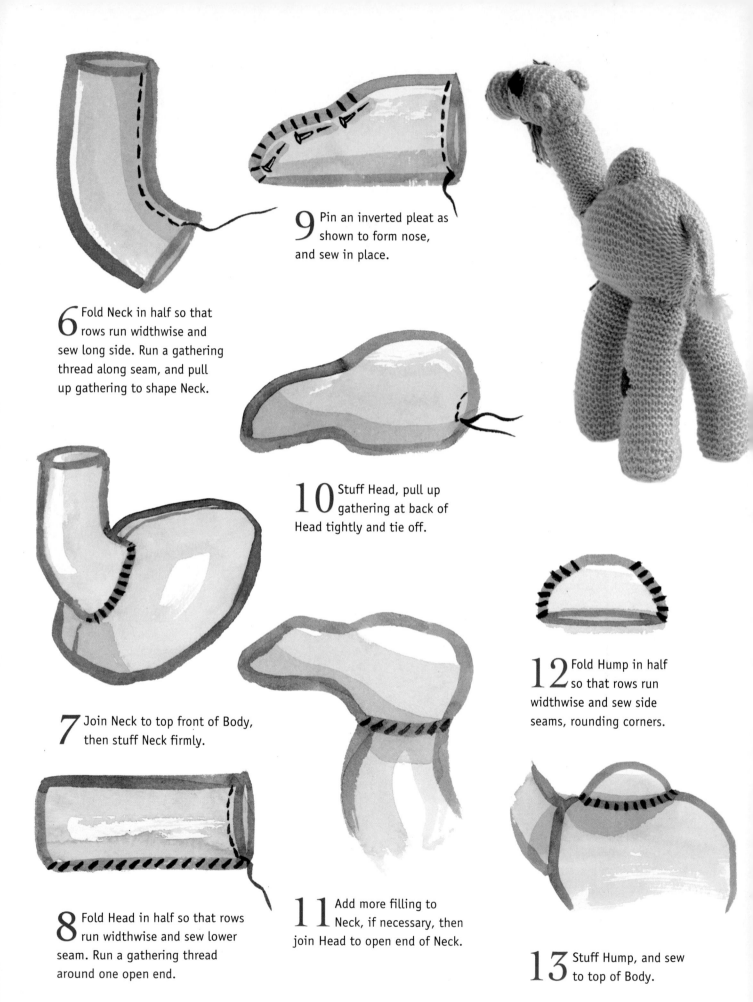

9 Pin an inverted pleat as shown to form nose, and sew in place.

6 Fold Neck in half so that rows run widthwise and sew long side. Run a gathering thread along seam, and pull up gathering to shape Neck.

10 Stuff Head, pull up gathering at back of Head tightly and tie off.

7 Join Neck to top front of Body, then stuff Neck firmly.

12 Fold Hump in half so that rows run widthwise and sew side seams, rounding corners.

8 Fold Head in half so that rows run widthwise and sew lower seam. Run a gathering thread around one open end.

11 Add more filling to Neck, if necessary, then join Head to open end of Neck.

13 Stuff Hump, and sew to top of Body.

16 For tail, cut six lengths of blue yarn, each approximately 30cm, and hook them over a pin. Divide strands into three groups of four, and plait to a length of approximately 7cm. Tie off, trim ends into a tassel and sew tail to back of Body.

14 Run a gathering thread around each Knee. Pull up gathering and pin a Knee onto each Leg, folding edges under to create rounded shape. Sew in place.

17 For nose and neck bands, using a variety of coloured yarns, plait a length to fit around nose and one to fit around neck. Leave some unplaited yarn at either end of each band for tassel. Using matching yarn, secure bands around nose and neck. For a thicker tassel, cut several lengths of coloured yarns and attach to top of tassel with a slip knot.

15 Run a gathering thread along one long side of each Ear and pull up gathers. Join gathered edge of each Ear to side of Head.

18 Work brown nostrils and black eyes in satin stitch. Thread needle with a length of black yarn, pull it through above eye, and knot strands firmly. Continue knotting black yarn around tops of eyes, then trim eyelashes to approximately 1cm, unravelling strands to make them fluffy.

MEASUREMENTS

Approximately 42cm tall.

MATERIALS

8-ply acrylic yarn (50g):

- ■ Two balls grey
- ■ Small amounts yellow, white, black, and white bouclé
- ■ Small amount red, for embroidery
- ■ One pair 4mm (No 8) knitting needles
- ■ Knitter's needle, for sewing seams and embroidery
- ■ Polyester filling
- ■ Ribbon

KNITTING

Note: *Before beginning, it is important to read the* **Basic Instructions** *on page 5.*

Approximately 48 rows

HEAD
make 2

28 stitches

Using grey, cast on 28 sts.
Knit 48 rows, cast off.

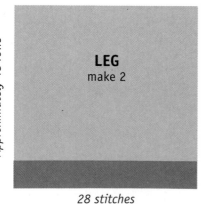

Approximately 48 rows

LEG
make 2

28 stitches

Using grey, cast on 28 sts.
Knit 42 rows. Change to black,
knit 6 rows, cast off.

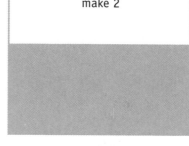

Approximately 48 rows

EAR
make 2

28 stitches

Using white bouclé, cast on 28 sts.
Knit 24 rows. Change to grey,
knit 24 rows, cast off.

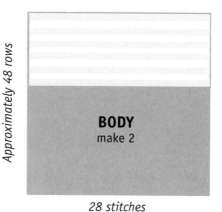

Approximately 48 rows

BODY
make 2

28 stitches

Using yellow, cast on 28 sts. Knit 22
rows in stripes of 2 rows yellow and 2
rows white, ending with a yellow row.
Change to grey, knit 26 rows, cast off.

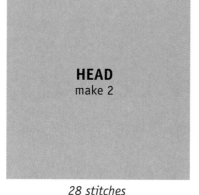

Approximately 48 rows

ARM
make 2

28 stitches

Using yellow, cast on 28 sts. Knit 22
rows in stripes of 2 rows yellow and
2 rows white, ending with a yellow
row. Change to grey, knit 20 rows.
Change to black, knit 6 rows, cast off.

TO MAKE UP

1 Matching stripes, join Body squares together along three sides, leaving neck and shoulder edge open.

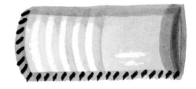

2 Fold each Arm in half, matching stripes, and join along cast-on edge and long side.

3 Fold each Leg in half, and join along cast-on edge and long side.

Koala

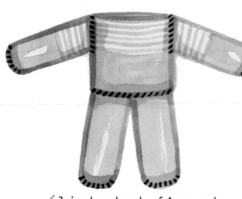

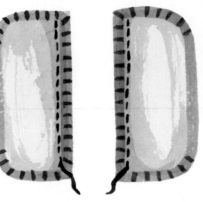

4 Join closed ends of Arms and Legs to Body. Stuff Arms and Legs with polyester filling and sew open ends closed, rounding corners. Stuff Body.

8 Insert neck in centre of Body opening, pin then sew neck to neck edge of Body. Add more filling to Body, if necessary, and sew shoulder seams.

9 Fold each Ear in half along colour change and sew around three sides, rounding corners. Run a gathering thread along sewn edge.

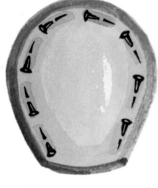

5 Pin Head squares together, rounding corners and shaping neck.

6 Sew around edge, leaving neck edge open for stuffing.

10 Join gathered edge of each Ear to Head seam, with white half of Ear at front. Fold down the top of each Ear to the front and catch with a few stitches.

7 Run a gathering thread around neck edge and top of neck. Stuff Head, pull up neck gathering to approximately 20cm, and stuff neck.

11 Using black, work eyes and nose in satin stitch, building up several layers for the nose. Using a double red thread, work mouth in couching stitch or stem stitch. Tie a ribbon around Koala's neck to finish.

Snake

MEASUREMENTS

Approximately 18cm in diameter x desired length (our Snake is 210cm long).

MATERIALS

8-ply acrylic yarn (50g):
- Leftover yarns of any colour — we used lots of different colours, but you could make a Snake in different shades of the one colour
- Small amounts pink and green
- One pair 4mm (No 8) knitting needles
- Knitter's needle, for sewing seams and embroidery
- Polyester filling

KNITTING

Note: *Before beginning, it is important to read the **Basic Instructions** on page 5.*

Approximately 48 rows

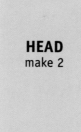

MOUTH
make 1

HEAD
make 2

14 stitches

14 stitches

Using pink for Mouth and green for Head, cast on 14 sts. Knit 48 rows, cast off.

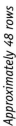
Approximately 48 rows

BODY
make as many as desired

Approximately 48 rows

TAIL
make 1

28 stitches

Using colour of choice, cast on 28 sts. Knit 48 rows in random stripe pattern, using colours of choice (or knit square in one colour), cast off.

14 stitches

Using colour of choice, cast on 14 sts. Knit 48 rows in random stripe pattern, using colours of choice, cast off.

TO MAKE UP

a

a

b

b

1 Join Body squares together to form long strip (a), joining Tail piece to one end (b).

2 Fold Body in half lengthwise, and sew long seam (a), folding in Tail end to create a point (b) and leaving openings along length for stuffing. Stuff Body with polyester filling, closing openings as you progress. Set aside.

3 For tongue, cut three strands of red yarn, each approximately 50cm, and hook them over a large pin. Divide strands into three groups of two, and plait to a length of about 12cm.

5 Thread other end of tongue through centre of Mouth piece, and sew in place.

7 Pin one half of Mouth piece to pinned end of one Head piece, shaping Mouth to match Head. Pin other half of Mouth to pinned end of other Head piece. Sew when satisfied with shape.

8 Sew side seams of Head, and stuff.

6 Fold under corners of one end of each Head piece to form mouth shape, and pin.

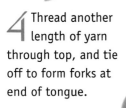

4 Thread another length of yarn through top, and tie off to form forks at end of tongue.

9 Join Head to Body. Work eyes in satin stitch. If desired, thread lengths of different coloured yarn through stitches around circumference of your Snake for decoration.

Mermaid

MEASUREMENTS

Approximately 51cm long.

MATERIALS

8-ply acrylic yarn (50g):

- Two balls pale blue
- One ball variegated
- One ball pale aqua, for hair and topknot
- Small amounts dark brown, pink, deep red, yellow and white, for embroidery
- One pair 4mm (No 8) knitting needles
- Knitter's needle, for sewing seams and embroidery
- Polyester filling

KNITTING

Note: *Before beginning, it is important to read the **Basic Instructions** on page 5.*

Approximately 48 rows

HEAD
make 2

ARM
make 2

28 stitches

Approximately 48 rows

LOWER BODY
make 2

TAIL
make 1

28 stitches

Using pale blue for Head and Arms, and variegated for Lower Body and Tail, cast on 28 sts.
Knit 48 rows, cast off.

Approximately 48 rows

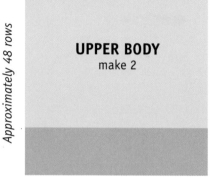

UPPER BODY
make 2

28 stitches

Using pale blue, cast on 28 sts.
Knit 32 rows. Change to variegated, knit 16 rows, cast off.

TO MAKE UP

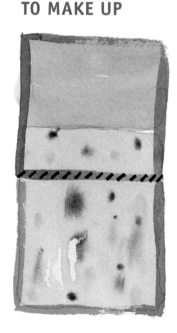

1 Join each Upper Body to a Lower Body along variegated edges, to form two body pieces.

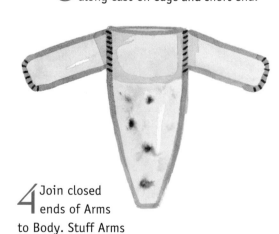

2 Join body pieces together, shaping Lower Body as shown and leaving neck and shoulder edge open.

3 Fold each Arm in half, and join along cast-on edge and short end.

4 Join closed ends of Arms to Body. Stuff Arms with polyester filling and sew open ends closed, rounding corners. Stuff Body.

5 Pin Head squares together, rounding corners and shaping neck.

6 Sew around edge, leaving neck edge open for stuffing.

7 Run a gathering thread around neck edge and top of neck. Stuff Head, pull up neck gathering to approximately 19cm, and stuff neck.

8 Insert neck in centre of Body opening, pin then sew neck to neck edge of Body. Add more filling to Body, if necessary, and sew shoulder seams.

9 Fold Tail in half diagonally and sew one seam, leaving about 1cm unsewn at corner. Stuff Tail and sew remaining seam, again leaving about 1cm unsewn.

10 Fold in unsewn corners of Tail and join this edge to Lower Body. Divide Tail in half with a vertical line of running stitch, pulling stitching slightly to create fishtail shape.

11 For hank of hair, using pale aqua yarn, make about 30 loops, each 50cm in length. Tie loops at centre, leaving tie ends extending. Repeat to make another three hanks. Using centre tie, sew one hank to centre of Mermaid's forehead. Sew remaining hanks to centre top of Head. Pull hair to either side of face, and secure hair at side and back of Head, at eye level, with backstitch.

12 For topknot, using pale aqua yarn, make approximately 30 loops, each about 7cm in length. Tie loops at centre, as for hank of hair, and sew topknot to top of Head.

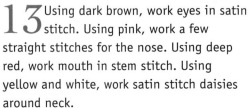

13 Using dark brown, work eyes in satin stitch. Using pink, work a few straight stitches for the nose. Using deep red, work mouth in stem stitch. Using yellow and white, work satin stitch daisies around neck.

MEASUREMENTS

Approximately 32cm high.

MATERIALS

8-ply acrylic yarn (50g):

- Two balls white (use bouclé if desired)
- One ball variegated, for scarf (optional)
- Small amounts black and red, for embroidery
- One pair 4mm (No 8) knitting needles
- Knitter's needle, for sewing seams and embroidery
- Polyester filling

KNITTING

Note: *Before beginning, it is important to read the* **Basic Instructions** *on page 5.*

Approximately 48 rows

SIDE/ LOWER BACK BODY
make 2
LEG
make 2

28 stitches

Using white, cast on 28 sts. Knit 48 rows, cast off.

Approximately 24 rows

SIDE/ TOP BACK BODY
make 2

28 stitches

Using white, cast on 28 sts. Knit 24 rows, cast off.

Approximately 24 rows

HEAD
make 2
TOP FRONT BODY
make 1
ARM
make 2

14 stitches

Using white, cast on 14 sts. Knit 24 rows, cast off.

Approximately 48 rows

LOWER FRONT BODY
make 1

14 stitches

Using white, cast on 14 sts. Knit 48 rows, cast off.

SCARF
make 1
(optional)

7 stitches

Using variegated, cast on 7 sts. Knit to length required, cast off.

TO MAKE UP

1 Join each Head to a Side/Top Back Body, then join to a Side/Lower Back Body, to form two side/back pieces.

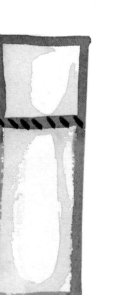

2 Join Top Front Body to Lower Front Body, to form front piece.

Polar Bear

3 Join side/back Head pieces together along centre front. Pin then sew front piece into opening below this seam, to form body piece.

4 Fold body piece along centre front.

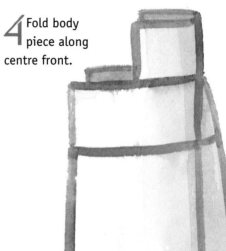

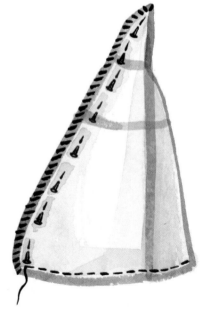

5 Pin centre back seam, folding under corners to create a smooth shape that tapers to a point at top of Head, and sew. Run a gathering thread around lower open edge of body.

6 Stuff body with polyester filling, pull up gathering and sew lower edge closed.

7 Fold each Leg in half diagonally, sew one seam and round two corners as shown (a). Stuff Leg and sew opening closed (b).

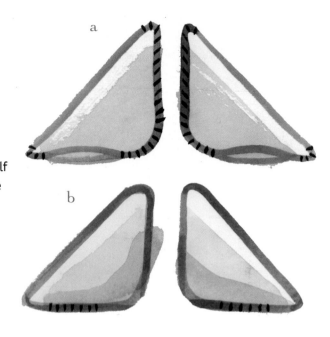

8 Fold each Arm in half diagonally and sew one seam (a). Stuff Arm and sew remaining seam (b).

9 Join each Arm to a top body seam, with folded edge of Arm uppermost and lower corner of Arm on seam between top and lower body. Join a Leg to each lower body seam, aligning lower surface of Leg with lower surface of body.

10 Using white, work a straight stitch (approximately 1cm long) on either side of Head to mark position of ears. Work two rows of buttonhole stitch over each straight stitch to form ears. Using black, embroider eyes in satin stitch, then make nose by stitching across point of head in one way, then across in the opposite direction, building up several layers. Using red, work two straight stitches for mouth. Using black, wrap ends of Arms for paws, then sew together. Repeat for Legs. Drape scarf around neck to finish, if desired.

MEASUREMENTS

Approximately 29cm long x 14cm high.

MATERIALS

8-ply acrylic yarn (50g):

- One ball each pale green and blue-green
- Small amounts green, bright green, aqua, red and black
- One pair 4mm (No 8) knitting needles
- Knitter's needle, for sewing seams and embroidery
- Polyester filling

KNITTING

Note: *Before beginning, it is important to read the* **Basic Instructions** *on page 5.*

Approximately 48 rows

BODY
make 2

Approximately 48 rows

LARGE WING
make 2

Approximately 48 rows

LARGE TAIL
make 1

28 stitches

Using pale green for Body, blue-green for Large Wing and aqua for Large Tail, cast on 28 sts. Knit 48 rows, cast off.

Approximately 12 rows

FOOT
make 2

14 stitches

Using black, cast on 14 sts. Knit 12 rows, cast off.

Approximately 48 rows

SMALL TAIL
make 1

14 stitches

Using pale green, cast on 14 sts. Knit 14 rows, change to blue-green, knit 6 rows. Change to green, knit 2 rows. Change to aqua, knit 4 rows. Change to blue-green, knit 22 rows, cast off.

Approximately 24 rows

SMALL WING
make 2

14 stitches

Using green, cast on 14 sts. Knit 8 rows, change to aqua, knit 8 rows. Change to bright green, knit 8 rows, cast off.

Approximately 12 rows

CROWN
make 1

7 stitches

BEAK
make 1

7 stitches

Using bright green for Crown and red for Beak, cast on 7 sts. Knit 12 rows, cast off.

TO MAKE UP

1 Pin then sew Body squares together, folding in lower front corner as shown and leaving lower edge open for stuffing.

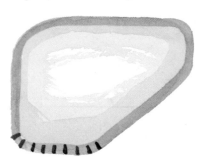

2 Stuff Body with polyester filling and sew lower edge closed.

3 Fold each Large Wing in half diagonally, one with wrong sides together and one with right sides together, and sew seams.

Tropical Bird

4 Fold each Small Wing in half diagonally, one with wrong sides together and one with right sides together, and sew seams.

5 Position each Small Wing on top of a Large Wing, aligning folded edges. Sew in place, leaving small section unsewn.

6 Position wings on Body so that front corners are about 6cm from head end of Body and folded edges are aligned with top Body seam. Sew wings to seam for about 7cm, leaving back ends of wings free.

7 Fold Large Tail in half and sew side seam for about 6cm. Run a gathering thread around open top end.

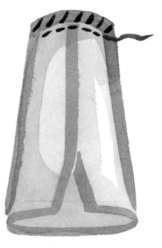

8 Arrange Large Tail so that seam lies in centre, pull up gathering slightly and sew gathered end closed.

9 Fold Small Tail in half widthwise and sew side seams. Run a gathering thread around open end.

10 Stuff Small Tail lightly, pull up gathering and sew gathered end closed.

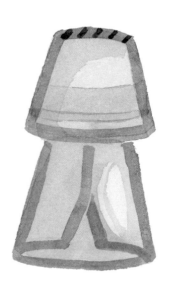

11 Join top of Small Tail to top of Large Tail.

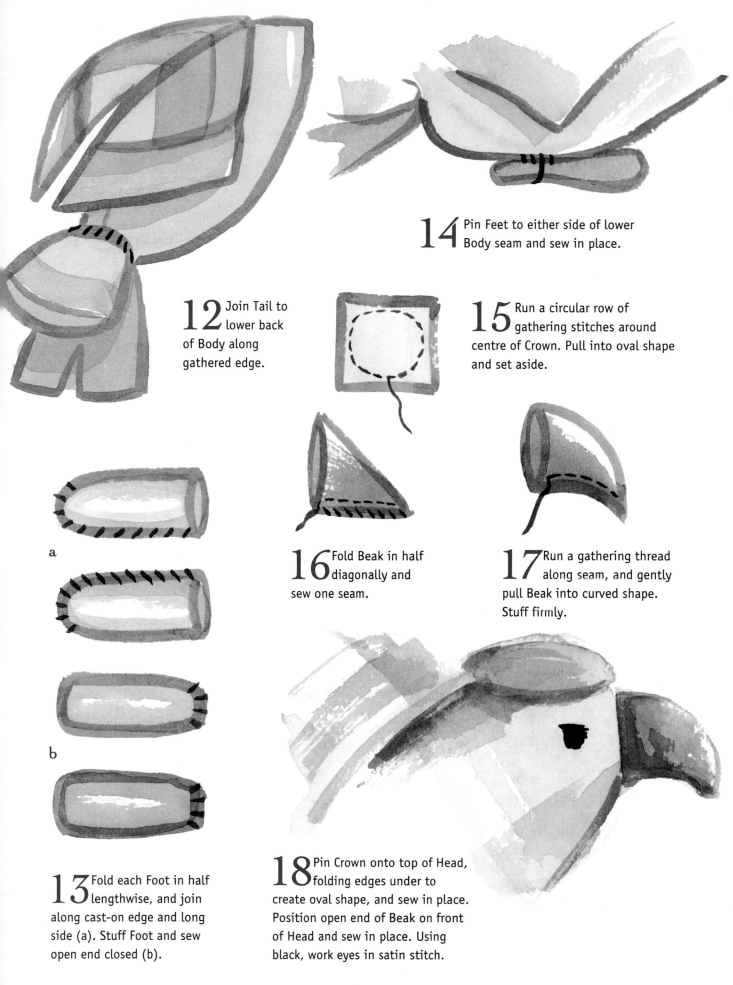

12 Join Tail to lower back of Body along gathered edge.

a

b

13 Fold each Foot in half lengthwise, and join along cast-on edge and long side (a). Stuff Foot and sew open end closed (b).

14 Pin Feet to either side of lower Body seam and sew in place.

15 Run a circular row of gathering stitches around centre of Crown. Pull into oval shape and set aside.

16 Fold Beak in half diagonally and sew one seam.

17 Run a gathering thread along seam, and gently pull Beak into curved shape. Stuff firmly.

18 Pin Crown onto top of Head, folding edges under to create oval shape, and sew in place. Position open end of Beak on front of Head and sew in place. Using black, work eyes in satin stitch.

MEASUREMENTS

Approximately 34cm high.

MATERIALS

8-ply acrylic yarn (50g):

- Two balls light brown
- Small amounts black and yellow
- Small amounts dark brown and orange, for embroidery
- One pair 4mm (No 8) knitting needles
- Knitter's needle, for sewing seams and embroidery
- Crochet hook, for mane and tail
- Polyester filling
- Small piece 20mm-wide cotton braid
- Small piece 5mm-wide patterned cord

KNITTING

Note: *Before beginning, it is important to read the* **Basic Instructions** *on page 5.*

Approximately 48 rows

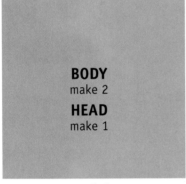

BODY
make 2

HEAD
make 1

28 stitches

Using light brown, cast on 28 sts. Knit 48 rows, cast off.

Approximately 48 rows

LEG
make 4

28 stitches

Using light brown, cast on 28 sts. Knit 42 rows. Change to black, knit 6 rows, cast off.

Approximately 12 rows

EAR
make 2

7 stitches

Using light brown, cast on 7 sts. Knit 12 rows, cast off.

TO MAKE UP

1 Join Body squares together along cast-on and cast-off edges, and run a gathering thread around open ends.

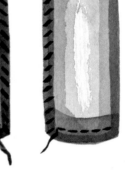

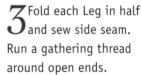

2 Pull up gathering to shape Body, and sew one end closed. Stuff Body with polyester filling, and sew remaining end closed.

3 Fold each Leg in half and sew side seam. Run a gathering thread around open ends.

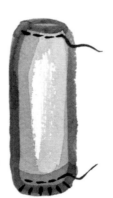

4 Pull up gathering around black (hoof) end of each Leg and sew opening closed. Stuff Legs. Pull up gathering slightly around remaining open end of each Leg.

Horse

5 Join open ends of Legs to Body, positioning two Legs either side of lower seam.

9 Join Head to top front of Body.

10 Fold in three corners of each Ear, and secure with a few stitches. Join Ears to top of Head.

6 Fold Head in half so that rows run widthwise and sew lower seam. Run a gathering thread around one open end.

7 Pin an inverted pleat as shown to form nose, and sew in place.

a

b

11 To make one of the tufts of the mane, cut eight lengths of yellow yarn, each approximately 25cm. Form one or two lengths into a loop and, using crochet hook, pull loop through a knitted stitch in top back half of Head (a). Thread ends through loop and pull to tighten knot (b). Repeat for remaining lengths in tuft. Make another nine tufts in same way, knotting them in a row along back of Head. When finished, trim mane to 4cm at front gradating to 7cm at back. Repeat for Tail, using 20 lengths of yellow yarn, each approximately 50cm.

8 Stuff Head, pull up gathering at back of Head tightly and tie off.

12 Sew braid around nose, for halter. Sew one end of cord to halter, take other end around back of head and sew to other side of halter. Using black, work eyes in satin stitch. Using dark brown, work nostrils in satin stitch. Using orange, work mouth in straight stitch.

Clown

MEASUREMENTS

Approximately 49cm tall.

MATERIALS

8-ply acrylic yarn (50g):

- One ball white
- Small amount each of different colours (we used approximately 25 colours)
- Novelty yarn, for Hair
- Small amounts red, pink and navy, for embroidery
- One pair 4mm (No 8) knitting needles
- Knitter's needle, for sewing seams and embroidery
- Old stockings or pantihose, for Leg Inserts
- Polyester filling
- 13cm x 130cm sheer print, for Frill

KNITTING

Note: *Before beginning, it is important to read the **Basic Instructions** on page 5.*

Our Clown features diagonally striped squares, which are knitted as follows:

Using colour of choice, cast on 2 sts. Knit 1 row. Knitting in stripes of any width and colour, increase 1 st at beginning of every row until there are 41 sts (approximately). Measure one side — it should be the same length as one side of the largest plain square. Now decrease 1 st (by knitting 2 sts together) at beginning of every row until there is 1 st remaining. Cast off.

Approximately 48 rows

HEAD
make 2

28 stitches

Using white, cast on 28 sts. Knit 48 rows, cast off.

Approximately 48 rows

YOKE
make 1

ARM
make 2

PANTS LEG
make 8

28 stitches

Using colour of choice, cast on 28 sts. Knit 48 rows in stripes of any width and colour, cast off.

Approximately 12 rows

NOSE
make 1

CHEEK
make 2

POMPOM
make 5

7 stitches *7 stitches* *7 stitches*

Using red for Nose, pink for Cheeks and any colour for Pompoms, cast on 7 sts. Knit 12 rows, cast off.

Approximately 24 rows

SHOE
make 2

28 stitches

Using colour of choice, cast on 28 sts. Knit 24 rows in same colour or in stripes of any width and colour, cast off.

Approximately 24 rows

HAND
make 2

14 stitches

Using white, cast on 14 sts. Knit 24 rows, cast off.

TO MAKE UP

1 Fold Yoke in half widthwise and sew side seams, leaving neck and shoulder edge open. Run a gathering thread along each seam.

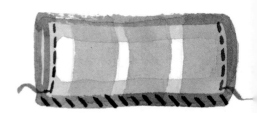

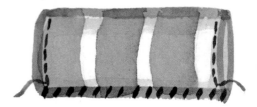

2 Fold each Arm in half, matching stripes if necessary, and sew long seam. Run a gathering thread around open ends.

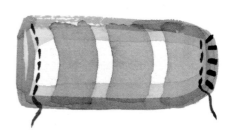

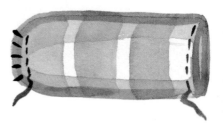

3 Pull up gathering slightly around one end of each Arm and sew opening closed.

4 Pull up gathering on Yoke, then join closed ends of Arms to Yoke. Stuff Arms with polyester filling, pull up gathering around open ends and sew openings closed.

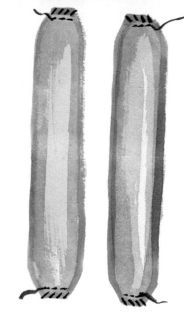

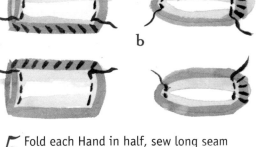

a

b

5 Fold each Hand in half, sew long seam and run a gathering thread around open ends (a). Pull up gathering at one end and tie off. Stuff Hand, pull up gathering at remaining end and sew opening closed (b).

7 For Leg Inserts, cut legs of a pair of old pantihose to same length as Pants (see step 9), and run a gathering thread around open ends. Stuff each Leg Insert, pull up gathering and sew openings closed.

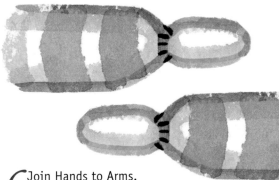

6 Join Hands to Arms.

8 Join Leg Inserts to lower edge of Yoke.

9 Join Pants Leg squares together in two groups of four.

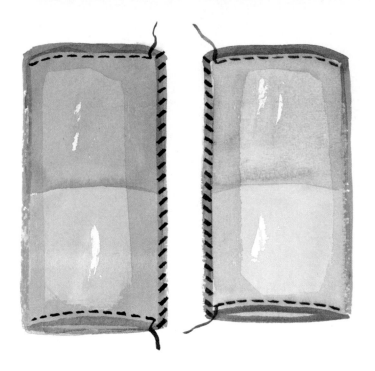

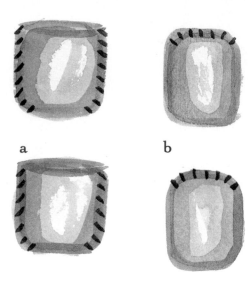

12 Fold each Shoe in half widthwise and sew side seams, rounding corners (a). Stuff Shoe and sew open end closed, rounding corners (b).

a

b

10 Fold each Pants Leg in half and sew side seam. Run a gathering thread around open ends.

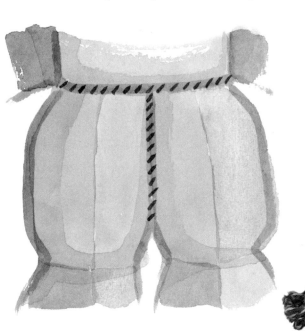

13 First join each Leg Insert and then join each Pants Leg to a Shoe, pulling up gathering around each Leg end before sewing.

11 Pull a Pants Leg over each Stocking Insert and adjust so that seams run down centre front and centre back. Pull up gathering at top edge of each Pants Leg — the Legs should fit across lower edge of Yoke — and sew to Yoke. Sew Pants together along inside Legs, beginning at the top and finishing about one-third of the way down.

14 Pin Head squares together, rounding corners and shaping neck.

15 Sew around edge, leaving neck edge open for stuffing.

18 Join ends of Ruffle together to form a ring.

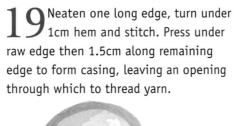

19 Neaten one long edge, turn under 1cm hem and stitch. Press under raw edge then 1.5cm along remaining edge to form casing, leaving an opening through which to thread yarn.

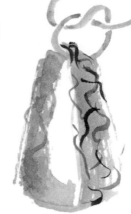

21 For hair tuft, using novelty yarn, make about 30 loops, each 20cm in length. Tie loops at centre with a strand of yarn. Repeat to make other hair tuft. Using centre tie, sew tufts to either side of Head.

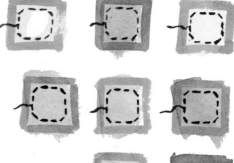

16 Run a gathering thread around neck edge and top of neck. Stuff Head, and pull up neck gathering to approximately 15cm (do not stuff neck).

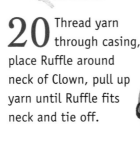

20 Thread yarn through casing, place Ruffle around neck of Clown, pull up yarn until Ruffle fits neck and tie off.

22 Run a gathering thread around Pompoms, Nose and Cheeks. Draw up gathering slightly. Stuff Pompoms and Nose with polyester filling, pull up gathering tightly and tie off.

17 Stuff Yoke. Insert neck in centre of Yoke opening, pin then sew neck to neck edge of Yoke. Add more filling to Yoke, if necessary, and sew shoulder seams.

23 Sew a Pompom to each Shoe, and the remaining three Pompoms to centre seam of Pants. Sew Nose and Cheeks to face, folding under edges of each Cheek to form oval shape. Using navy, work eyes in cross stitch and eyebrows in straight stitch. Using a double red thread, work mouth in straight stitch.

MEASUREMENTS

Approximately 64cm tall, including ears.

MATERIALS

8-ply acrylic yarn (50g):

- ■ Two balls white
- ■ One ball red
- ■ Small amounts white bouclé, orange and bright green
- ■ Small amounts black and brown, for embroidery
- ■ One pair 4mm (No 8) knitting needles
- ■ Knitter's needle, for sewing seams and embroidery
- ■ Polyester filling

KNITTING

Note: *Before beginning, it is important to read the **Basic Instructions** on page 5.*

TO MAKE UP RABBIT

1 Matching stripes, join Body squares together along three sides, leaving neck and shoulder edge open.

2 Fold each Arm in half, matching stripes, and join along cast-on edge and long side.

3 Fold each Leg in half, and join along cast-on edge and long side. Run a gathering thread around open end.

Approximately 48 rows

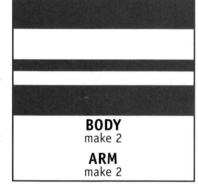

BODY
make 2

ARM
make 2

28 stitches

Using red, cast on 28 sts. Knit 28 rows in stripes of 6 rows red, 8 rows white, 4 rows red, 4 rows white and 6 rows red. Change to white, knit 20 rows, cast off.

Approximately 48 rows

HEAD
make 2

EAR
make 2

LEG
make 2

FOOT
make 2

TAIL
make 1

28 stitches

CARROT
make 1

28 stitches

Using white for Head, Ears, Legs and Feet, white bouclé for Tail, and orange for Carrot, cast on 28 sts. Knit 48 rows, cast off.

4 Join closed ends of Arms and Legs to Body. Stuff Arms with polyester filling and sew open ends closed, rounding corners. Stuff Legs and pull up gathering slightly. Stuff Body.

Rabbit

5 Fold each Foot in half, and join along cast-on edge and long side, rounding corners — fold in excess at end to shorten Foot, if necessary. Run a gathering thread around open end (a). Stuff Foot, pull up gathering and sew open end closed (b).

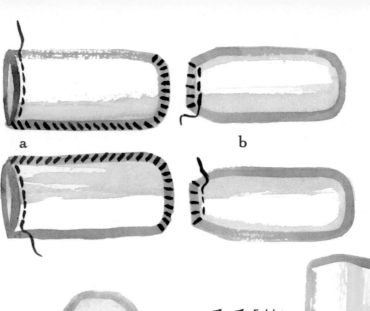

a

b

11 Fold each Ear in half and sew long seam.

6 Join each Foot to a Leg, adjusting gathering around Leg end, if necessary. Using black, work toes in straight stitch.

9 Run a gathering thread around neck edge and top of neck. Stuff Head, pull up neck gathering to approximately 22cm, and stuff neck.

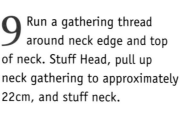

12 Arrange each Ear so that seam lies in centre, and sew one end of Ear closed, rounding corners. Stuff lightly.

7 Pin Head squares together, shaping as shown.

8 Sew around edge, leaving neck edge open for stuffing.

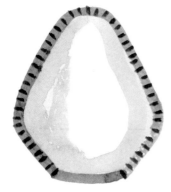

10 Insert neck in centre of Body opening, pin then sew neck to neck edge of Body. Add more filling to Body, if necessary, and sew shoulder seams.

13 With seam at back, fold each Ear as shown, and secure with a few stitches. Join Ears to top of Head.

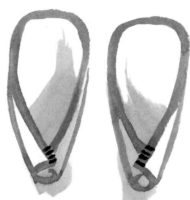

14 Run a gathering thread around Tail square.

15 Pull up gathering to create pouch, stuff Tail, pull up gathering tightly and tie off. Join Tail to lower Body.

16 Using black, work nose in satin stitch and whiskers in straight stitch. Using brown, work eyes in satin stitch and mouth in backstitch.

TO MAKE UP CARROT

17 Fold Carrot square in half diagonally and sew one seam. Run a gathering thread around open end.

18 Stuff Carrot, pull up gathering and tie off. Knot lengths of green yarn through top of Carrot.

MEASUREMENTS

Approximately 50cm tall.

MATERIALS

8-ply acrylic yarn (50g):

- Two balls pink
- Small amounts black and white
- Small amount red, for embroidery
- One ball green, for Waistcoat
- Small amount metallic (optional), for Waistcoat
- One pair 4mm (No 8) knitting needles
- Knitter's needle, for sewing seams and embroidery
- Polyester filling
- Ribbon

KNITTING

Note: *Before beginning, it is important to read the* **Basic Instructions** *on page 5.*

Approximately 55 rows

WAISTCOAT BACK
make 1

35 stitches

Using green, cast on 35 sts. Knit 55 rows, cast off.

Approximately 55 rows

WAISTCOAT FRONT
make 2

18 stitches

Using green, cast on 18 sts. Knit 25 rows, change to metallic. Knit 30 rows in stripes of 4 rows metallic, 6 rows green, ending with a green row, cast off.

Approximately 48 rows

TRUNK
make 1

14 stitches

Using pink, cast on 14 sts. Knit 48 rows, cast off.

Approximately 12 rows

TUSK
make 2

TAIL
make 1

7 stitches *7 stitches*

Using white for Tusks and pink for Tail, cast on 7 sts. Knit 12 rows, cast off.

Approximately 48 rows

HEAD
make 2
BODY
make 2

28 stitches

Using pink, cast on 28 sts. Knit 48 rows, cast off.

Approximately 24 rows

EAR
make 2

28 stitches

Using pink, cast on 28 sts. Knit 24 rows, cast off.

Approximately 48 rows

ARM
make 2
LEG
make 2

28 stitches

Using pink, cast on 28 sts. Knit 40 rows. Change to black, knit 8 rows, cast off.

Elephant

TO MAKE UP ELEPHANT

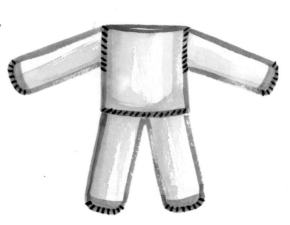

1 Join Body squares together along three sides, leaving neck and shoulder edge open.

3 Join closed ends of Arms and Legs to Body. Stuff Arms and Legs with polyester filling and sew open ends closed, rounding corners. Stuff Body.

6 Run a gathering thread around neck edge and top of neck. Stuff Head, pull up neck gathering to approximately 20cm, and stuff neck.

4 Pin Head squares together, rounding corners and shaping neck.

7 Insert neck in centre of Body opening, pin then sew neck to neck edge of Body. Add more filling to Body, if necessary, and sew shoulder seams.

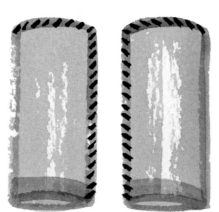

2 Fold each Arm and Leg in half, and join along cast-on edge and long side.

5 Sew around edge, leaving neck edge open for stuffing.

8 Run a gathering thread along one long side of each Ear, and pull up slightly. Turn down top corner of Ear and secure with a few stitches.

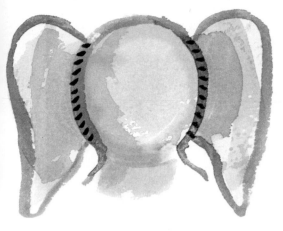

13 Fold each Tusk and the Tail square in half diagonally and sew one seam.

9 Attach gathered side of each Ear to Head seam.

a   b

14 Arrange each Tusk and the Tail so that seam lies in centre (a), tuck lower corner up inside lower edge and sew along lower edge (b).

10 Fold Trunk piece in half lengthwise and sew long seam, folding in one end to create a point.

15 Fold each Tusk and the Tail again and sew seam.

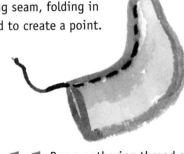

11 Run a gathering thread along seam and gently pull Trunk into shape shown. Stuff Trunk firmly, adjusting gathering to maintain shape.

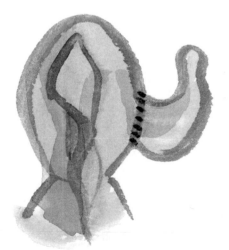

12 Position Trunk on lower half of face and sew in place.

16 Position Tail on lower back of Body and sew in place. Position Tusks on either side of Trunk and sew in place. Using black, work eyes in satin stitch. Using red, work mouth in straight stitch. Tie a ribbon around Elephant's neck.

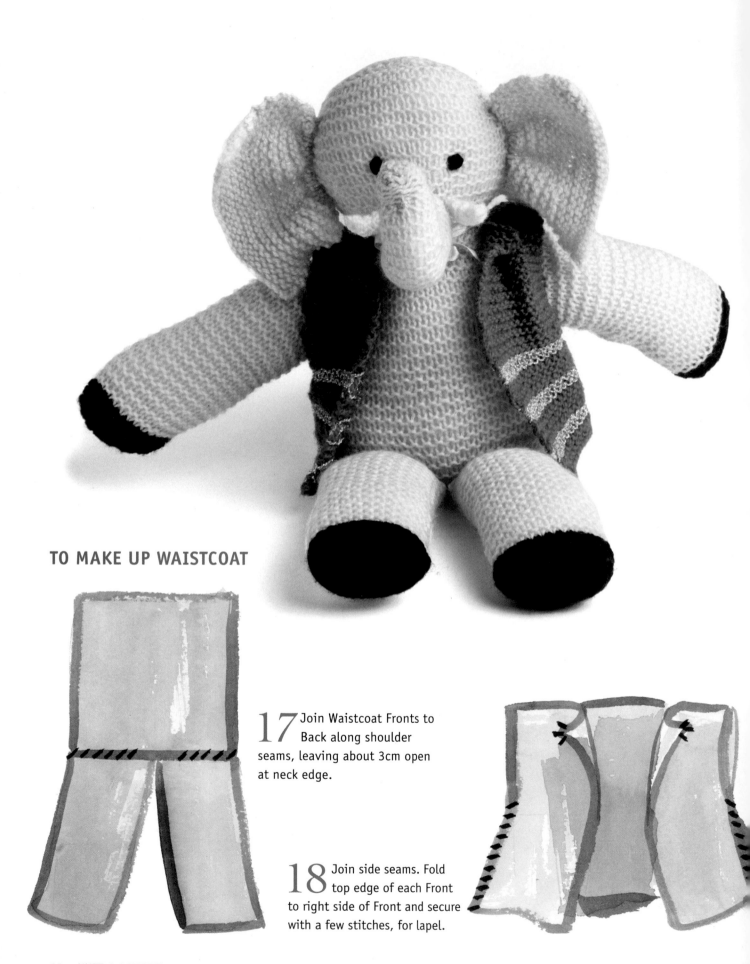

TO MAKE UP WAISTCOAT

17 Join Waistcoat Fronts to Back along shoulder seams, leaving about 3cm open at neck edge.

18 Join side seams. Fold top edge of each Front to right side of Front and secure with a few stitches, for lapel.

Dog

MEASUREMENTS

Approximately 44cm long.

MATERIALS

8-ply acrylic yarn (50g):

- Two balls white
- Small amounts black and pink
- Small amounts red and aqua, for embroidery
- One pair 4mm (No 8) knitting needles
- One pair 2.75mm (No 12) knitting needles
- Knitter's needle, for sewing seams and embroidery
- Polyester filling
- Small collar (optional)

KNITTING

Note: *Before beginning, it is important to read the* **Basic Instructions** *on page 5.*

Approximately 48 rows

BODY
make 2

LEG
make 4

28 stitches

Using 4mm needles and white, cast on 28 sts. Knit 48 rows, cast off.

Approximately 24 rows

HEAD
make 1

28 stitches

Using 4mm needles and white, cast on 28 sts. Knit 24 rows, cast off.

Approximately 12 rows

EAR
make 2

7 stitches

Using 4mm needles and white, cast on 7 sts. Knit 12 rows, cast off.

Approximately 12 rows

TONGUE
make 1

7 stitches

Using 2.75mm needles and pink, cast on 7 sts. Knit 12 rows in stocking stitch (see page 95), cast off.

Approximately 24 rows

TAIL
make 1

Approximately 24 rows

SPOT
make 6
or more

14 stitches

Using 4 mm needles and white for Tail and black for Spots, cast on 14 sts. Knit 24 rows, cast off.

TO MAKE UP

1 Join Body squares together along three sides.

2 Stuff Body with polyester filling, and sew open end closed.

3 Fold each Leg in half so that rows run widthwise and sew side seam. Run a gathering thread around one open end.

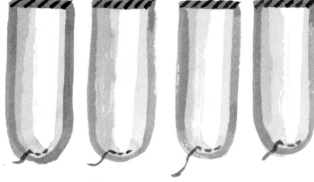

4 Pull up gathering and tie off. Stuff each Leg, and sew open end closed.

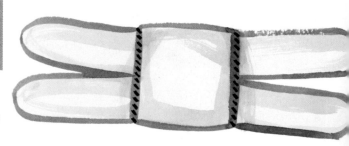

5 Join ungathered ends of Legs to front and back seams of Body, making sure that rows on Body and Legs run in same direction.

6 Fold Head in half widthwise. Pin then sew around edges, shaping nose and top of Head as shown, and leaving neck edge open. Stuff Head.

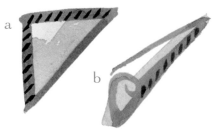

7 Join open neck edge of Head to top front of Body.

8 Fold Tail piece in half diagonally and sew seams (a). Roll lengthwise and stitch long seam (b).

9 Position Tail on top of Body, just above back seam, and sew in place.

10 Run a gathering thread around each Spot, pull up gathering — tightly for small Spots and loosely for large Spots — and sew Spots to Body.

11 Fold in three corners of each Ear, and secure with a few stitches. Join Ears to top of Head.

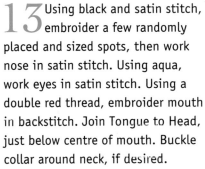

12 Fold Tongue in half so that rows run lengthwise and join along three sides, rounding corners of one end.

13 Using black and satin stitch, embroider a few randomly placed and sized spots, then work nose in satin stitch. Using aqua, work eyes in satin stitch. Using a double red thread, embroider mouth in backstitch. Join Tongue to Head, just below centre of mouth. Buckle collar around neck, if desired.

MEASUREMENTS

Approximately 40cm high, including antlers.

MATERIALS

8-ply acrylic yarn (50g):

- ■ Two balls dark brown
- ■ Small amounts black, white and beige
- ■ Small amounts red and yellow, for embroidery
- ■ One pair 4mm (No 8) knitting needles
- ■ Knitter's needle, for sewing seams and embroidery
- ■ Beige sewing thread
- ■ Polyester filling
- ■ Small piece 10mm-wide braid
- ■ Small piece 5mm-wide braid

KNITTING

Note: *Before beginning, it is important to read the* **Basic Instructions** *on page 5.*

Approximately 48 rows

BODY
make 2

HEAD
make 1

28 stitches

Using dark brown, cast on 28 sts.
Knit 48 rows, cast off.

Approximately 48 rows

LEG
make 4

28 stitches

Using dark brown, cast on 28 sts.
Knit 42 rows. Change to black, knit 6 rows, cast off.

TO MAKE UP

1 Join Body squares together along cast-on and cast-off edges, and run a gathering thread around open ends.

2 Pull up gathering to shape Body, and sew one end closed. Stuff Body with polyester filling, and sew remaining end closed.

Approximately 24 rows

ANTLER
make 5

14 stitches

Using beige, cast on 14 sts. Knit 24 rows, cast off.

Approximately 12 rows

EAR
make 2
INNER TAIL
make 1

OUTER TAIL
make 1

7 stitches   *7 stitches*

Using dark brown for Ears and Inner Tail, and white for Outer Tail, cast on 7 sts. Knit 12 rows, cast off.

3 Fold each Leg in half and sew side seam. Run a gathering thread around open ends.

4 Pull up gathering around black (hoof) end of each Leg and sew opening closed. Stuff Legs. Pull up gathering slightly around remaining open end of each Leg.

Rudolph

5 Join open ends of Legs to Body, positioning two Legs either side of lower seam.

6 Fold Head in half so that rows run widthwise and sew lower seam. Run a gathering thread around one open end.

7 Pin an inverted pleat as shown to form nose, and sew in place.

8 Stuff Head, pull up gathering at back of Head tightly and tie off.

9 Join Head to top front of Body.

10 Fold in three corners of each Ear, and secure with a few stitches. Join Ears to top of Head.

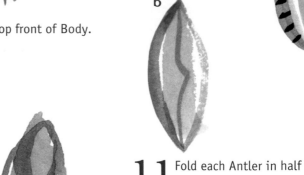

a

b

c

11 Fold each Antler in half diagonally and sew seams (a). Arrange Antler so that seams lie in centre (b), roll very tightly lengthwise and sew along edge (c).

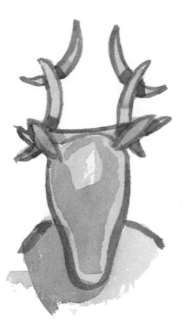

12 Sew Antlers together as shown, then join curved edge of central Antler to Head, positioning it just behind Ears.

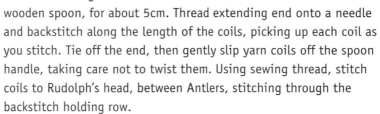

13 To make the mane, wind beige yarn around the end of a large wooden spoon, for about 5cm. Thread extending end onto a needle and backstitch along the length of the coils, picking up each coil as you stitch. Tie off the end, then gently slip yarn coils off the spoon handle, taking care not to twist them. Using sewing thread, stitch coils to Rudolph's head, between Antlers, stitching through the backstitch holding row.

14 Join Inner and Outer Tail pieces together, rounding opposing corners.

15 Join Tail to end of Body, with white (Outer) Tail at the back.

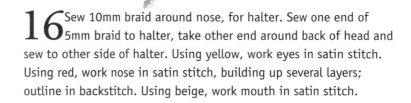

16 Sew 10mm braid around nose, for halter. Sew one end of 5mm braid to halter, take other end around back of head and sew to other side of halter. Using yellow, work eyes in satin stitch. Using red, work nose in satin stitch, building up several layers; outline in backstitch. Using beige, work mouth in satin stitch.

MEASUREMENTS

Approximately 27cm high.

MATERIALS

8-ply acrylic yarn (50g):

- One ball each apricot and grey-brown bouclé
- Small amounts black, grey-brown and red, for embroidery
- One pair 4mm (No 8) knitting needles
- Knitter's needle, for sewing seams and embroidery
- Polyester filling
- Ribbon

KNITTING

Note: *Before beginning, it is important to read the **Basic Instructions** on page 5.*

1 Join Front Body and Back Body together along sides, and run a gathering thread around open ends.

2 Pull up gathering to shape Body and sew lower edge closed (seam should be about 10cm long).

Approximately 48 rows

EAR
make 2

14 stitches

Using grey-brown, cast on 14 sts. Knit 24 rows. Change to apricot, knit 24 rows, cast off.

Approximately 48 rows

ARM
make 2
LEG
make 2

14 stitches

Using grey-brown, cast on 14 sts. Knit 38 rows. Change to apricot, knit 10 rows, cast off.

Approximately 96 rows

TAIL
make 1

14 stitches

Using grey-brown, cast on 14 sts. Knit 96 rows, cast off.

Approximately 24 rows

MUZZLE
make 1

28 stitches

Using apricot, cast on 28 sts. Knit 24 rows, cast off.

Approximately 48 rows

FRONT BODY
make 1

28 stitches

BACK BODY
make 1
HEAD
make 2

28 stitches

Using apricot for Front Body, and grey-brown for Back Body and Head, cast on 28 sts. Knit 48 rows, cast off.

Approximately 24 rows

FACE
make 1

14 stitches

Using apricot, cast on 14 sts. Knit 24 rows, cast off.

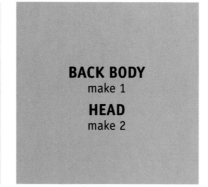

Monkey

3 Fold each Arm and Leg in half widthwise, and join along cast-on edge and long side. Run a gathering thread around open end.

5 Pin Head squares together, rounding corners and shaping neck.

8 Insert neck in Body opening, add more filling to Body if necessary, pull up gathering around neck edge of Body to fit neck, and tie off. Sew neck to neck edge of Body.

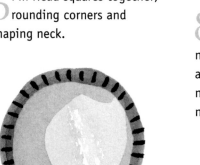

4 Join closed ends of Arms and Legs to Body. Stuff Arms and Legs with polyester filling, pull up gathering at ends and sew openings closed. Stuff Body.

6 Sew around edge, leaving neck edge open for stuffing.

9 Fold each Ear in half along colour change. Sew around three sides, folding in excess along straight side and rounding corners. Run a gathering thread along sewn edge.

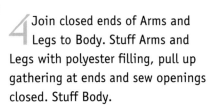

7 Run a gathering thread around neck edge and top of neck. Stuff Head, pull up gathering to approximately 19cm, and stuff neck.

10 Pull up gathering slightly and join gathered edge of each Ear to Head seam.

11 Run a circular row of gathering stitches around Face square.

12 Pull Face into oval shape and pin onto top front of Head, folding edges under, then sew in place.

13 Fold Muzzle in half widthwise, sew upper seam and run a gathering thread around one open end.

14 Pull up gathering tightly and tie off. Stuff Muzzle.

15 Position Muzzle on Head, overlapping Face slightly, and sew in place.

16 Fold Tail in half lengthwise and sew long seam, folding in one end to create a point. Stuff well, sew open end closed and join to lower half of back Body.

17 Using black, work eyes in satin stitch. Using grey-brown, work nose in satin stitch. Using a double red thread, work mouth in straight stitch. Tie a ribbon around Monkey's neck to finish.

MEASUREMENTS
Approximately 40cm tall.

MATERIALS
8-ply acrylic yarn (50g):
- One ball each cream, orange and purple
- Small amounts white and blue
- Small amounts red and dark brown, for embroidery
- One pair 4mm (No 8) knitting needles
- Knitter's needle, for sewing seams and embroidery
- Polyester filling

KNITTING
Note: *Before beginning, it is important to read the* **Basic Instructions** *on page 5*

TO MAKE UP

1 Pin then sew Head/Body squares together, folding in edges to create an egg shape and leaving lower edge open for stuffing. Run a gathering thread around opening.

2 Stuff Head/Body with polyester filling, pull up gathering and sew lower edge closed (seam should be about 10cm long).

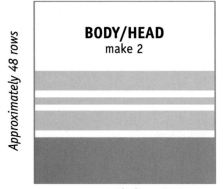

BODY/HEAD
make 2

Approximately 48 rows

28 stitches

Using cream, cast on 28 sts. Knit 20 rows. Change to orange, knit 16 rows in random stripe pattern, alternating orange and white. Change to purple, knit 12 rows, cast off.

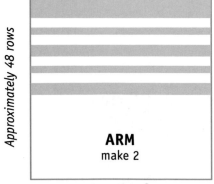

ARM
make 2

Approximately 48 rows

28 stitches

Using orange, cast on 28 sts. Knit 28 rows in random stripe pattern, alternating orange and white. Change to cream, knit 20 rows, cast off.

LEG
make 2

Approximately 48 rows

28 stitches

Using purple, cast on 28 sts. Knit 24 rows. Change to cream, knit 24 rows, cast off.

SHOE
make 2

Approximately 24 rows

28 stitches

Using blue, cast on 28 sts. Knit 24 rows, cast off.

3 Fold each Arm in half, matching stripes, and join along cast-on edge and long side. Run a gathering thread around open end.

Humpty

4 Join closed ends of Arms to Head/Body, level with striped section. Stuff Arms, pull up gathering around open ends and sew openings closed.

a

b

7 Fold each Shoe in half widthwise and sew side seams, rounding corners. Run a gathering thread around open end (a). Stuff Shoe, pull up gathering and sew open end closed (b).

5 Fold each Leg in half and sew side seam. Make a row of stitching following colour change, to suggest knee. Run a gathering thread around cream open end.

6 Stuff top section of each Leg and sew open end closed. Join top ends of Legs to lower front of Body, just below striped section. Stuff lower sections of Legs, and pull up gathering slightly.

8 Join each Shoe to a Leg, adjusting gathering around Leg end, if necessary. Using red, work laces in cross stitch.

9 Using dark brown, work eyes in satin stitch and eyebrows in straight stitch. Using a double red thread, work mouth in straight stitch.

Honey Bear

Approximately 26cm high.

MATERIALS

8-ply acrylic yarn (50g):

- One ball each dark brown and beige
- Small amount navy
- Small amounts black and yellow, for embroidery
- One pair 4mm (No 8) knitting needles
- Knitter's needle, for sewing seams and embroidery
- Polyester filling
- Ribbon

KNITTING

Note: *Before beginning, it is important to read the **Basic Instructions** on page 5.*

Approximately 24 rows

EAR
make 2

14 stitches

Using dark brown, cast on 14 sts. Knit 24 rows, cast off.

Approximately 48 rows

HEAD
make 1

14 stitches

Using dark brown, cast on 14 sts. Knit 48 rows, cast off.

Approximately 48 rows

FRONT BODY
make 1

28 stitches

BACK BODY
make 1

28 stitches

Using beige for Front Body and dark brown for Back Body, cast on 28 sts. Knit 48 rows, cast off.

Approximately 24 rows

ARM
make 2
LEG
make 2

28 stitches

Using dark brown, cast on 28 sts. Knit 16 rows. Change to navy, knit 8 rows, cast off.

Approximately 24 rows

MUZZLE
make 1

28 stitches

Using beige, cast on 28 sts. Knit 24 rows, cast off.

TO MAKE UP

1 Join Front Body and Back Body together along sides, and run a gathering thread around open ends.

2 Pull up gathering to shape Body and sew lower edge closed (seam should be about 10cm long).

3 Fold each Arm and Leg in half widthwise, and join along cast-on edge and long side.

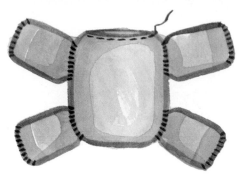

4 Join closed ends of Arms and Legs to Body. Stuff Arms and Legs with polyester filling and sew open ends closed, rounding corners. Stuff Body.

5 Fold Head square in half widthwise and pin sides together, rounding top corners and shaping neck.

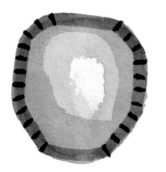

6 Sew along sides, leaving neck edge open for stuffing.

7 Run a gathering thread around neck edge and top of neck. Stuff Head, pull up neck gathering to approximately 18cm, and stuff neck.

8 Insert neck in Body opening, add more filling to Body if necessary, pull up gathering around neck edge of Body to fit neck, and tie off. Sew neck to neck edge of Body.

9 Fold each Ear in half and sew around three sides, rounding corners.

10 Join sewn edge of each Ear to Head seam.

11 Fold Muzzle in half widthwise, sew lower seam and run a gathering thread around one open end.

12 Pull up gathering tightly and tie off. Stuff Muzzle.

13 Position Muzzle on lower part of face and sew in place.

14 Using yellow, work eyes in satin stitch. Work a dark brown pupil over the top. Using black, work nose in satin stitch. Using dark brown, work mouth in stem stitch. Tie a ribbon around Bear's neck to finish.

MEASUREMENTS

Approximately 38cm high.

MATERIALS

8-ply acrylic yarn (50g):

- Two balls white bouclé
- Small amount pink
- Small amounts dark brown and black, for embroidery
- One pair 4mm (Size 8) knitting needles
- Knitter's needle, for sewing seams and embroidery
- Polyester filling
- Ribbon

KNITTING

Note: *Before beginning, it is important to read the **Basic Instructions** on page 5.*

HEAD
make 1

Approximately 48 rows

14 stitches

Using white, cast on 14 sts. Knit 48 rows, cast off.

BODY
make 2
LEG
make 4

Approximately 48 rows

28 stitches

Using white, cast on 28 sts. Knit 48 rows, cast off.

TAIL
make 1

Approximately 24 rows

28 stitches

Using white, cast on 28 sts. Knit 24 rows, cast off.

EAR
make 2

Approximately 24 rows

14 stitches

Using pink, cast on 14 sts. Knit 12 rows. Change to white, knit 12 rows, cast off.

TO MAKE UP

1 Join Body squares together, leaving openings as shown, and run a gathering thread around side opening.

2 Pull up gathering to shape Body, and sew side opening closed. Stuff Body with polyester filling.

3 Fold Head in half widthwise and pin sides together, rounding top corners and shaping neck.

4 Sew along sides, leaving neck edge open for stuffing.

5 Run a gathering thread around neck edge and top of neck. Stuff Head, pull up neck gathering to approximately 17cm, and stuff neck.

6 Insert neck in Body opening, pin then sew neck to neck edge of Body, completing back seam if necessary.

Lamb

9 Fold Tail in half lengthwise, shaping end as shown, and sew along side seam and short end.

11 Join Tail to Body.

10 Stuff Tail and sew open end closed, rounding corners.

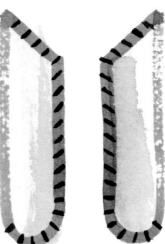

12 Fold each Ear in half along colour change and sew around three sides, rounding corners of one end and folding in other end diagonally as shown.

7 Fold each Leg in half and join along cast-on edge and long side. Stuff Legs.

8 Join open ends of Legs to Body, positioning two Legs either side of lower seam.

13 Join diagonally folded end of each Ear to Head seam, positioning Ear halfway down side of Head. Using dark brown, work eyes in satin stitch and mouth in backstitch. Using black, work nose in satin stitch, building up several layers. Tie a ribbon around Lamb's neck to finish.

Panda

MEASUREMENTS

Approximately 44cm tall.

MATERIALS

8-ply acrylic yarn (50g):

- Two balls black
- One ball white
- Small amounts yellow and red, for embroidery
- One pair 4mm (No 8) knitting needles
- Knitter's needle, for sewing seams and embroidery
- Polyester filling
- Ribbon

KNITTING

Note: *Before beginning, it is important to read the* **Basic Instructions** *on page 5.*

TO MAKE UP

1 Join Front Body and Back Body together along three sides, leaving neck and shoulder edge open.

2 Fold each Arm and Leg in half, and join along cast-on edge and long side.

Approximately 48 rows

BACK HEAD
make 1

BACK BODY
make 1

ARM
make 2

LEG
make 2

28 stitches

Using black, cast on 28 sts. Knit 48 rows, cast off.

Approximately 24 rows

EYE PATCH
make 2

EAR
make 2

14 stitches

Using black, cast on 14 sts. Knit 24 rows, cast off.

3 Join closed ends of Arms and Legs to Body. Stuff Arms and Legs with polyester filling and sew open ends closed, rounding corners slightly. Stuff Body.

Approximately 48 rows

FRONT HEAD
make 1

28 stitches

Using white, cast on 28 sts. Knit 48 rows, cast off.

Approximately 48 rows

FRONT BODY
make 1

28 stitches

Using black, cast on 28 sts. Knit 22 rows. Change to white, knit 26 rows, cast off.

4 Pin Head squares together, rounding corners and shaping neck.

5 Sew around edge, leaving neck edge open for stuffing.

6 Run a gathering thread around neck edge and top of neck. Stuff Head, pull up gathering to approximately 20cm, and stuff neck.

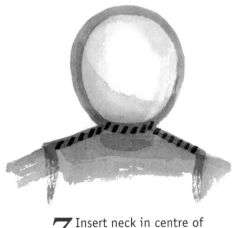

7 Insert neck in centre of Body opening, pin then sew neck to neck edge of Body. Add more filling to Body, if necessary, and sew shoulder seams.

8 Fold each Ear in half diagonally and sew around edge, rounding corners.

9 Join folded edge of each Ear to Head seam.

10 Run a diamond-shaped row of gathering stitches around each Eye Patch.

11 Pull up gathering and pin Eye Patches onto face, folding edges under to create rounded diamond shapes shown. Sew in place. Using yellow, work eyes in satin stitch. Using black, work nose in satin stitch. Using a double red thread, work mouth in couching stitch. Tie a ribbon around Panda's neck to finish.

MEASUREMENTS

Approximately 30cm long x 22cm high, including ears.

MATERIALS

8-ply acrylic yarn (50g):
- ■ Two balls pink
- ■ Small amounts navy and deep red, for embroidery
- ■ One pair 4mm (No 8) knitting needles
- ■ Knitter's needle, for sewing seams and embroidery
- ■ Polyester filling
- ■ Ribbon

KNITTING

Note: *Before beginning, it is important to read the **Basic Instructions** on page 5.*

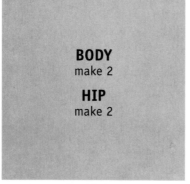

Approximately 48 rows

BODY
make 2

HIP
make 2

28 stitches

Cast on 28 sts, knit 48 rows, cast off.

Approximately 24 rows

HEAD
make 1

28 stitches

Cast on 28 sts, knit 24 rows, cast off.

Approximately 24 rows

make 7
SEE RIGHT

14 stitches

Cast on 14 sts, knit 24 rows, cast off.

FRONT LEG
make 2

BACK LEG
make 2

EAR
make 2

TAIL
make 1

TO MAKE UP

1 Join Body squares together along cast-on and cast-off edges, and run a gathering thread around open ends.

2 Pull up gathering to shape Body, and sew one end closed. Stuff Body with polyester filling, and sew remaining end closed.

3 Fold Head in half widthwise and sew lower seam. Run a gathering thread around one open end.

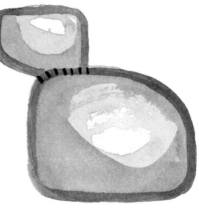

4 Pull up gathering to create muzzle shape, and sew muzzle end closed. Stuff Head and sew remaining end closed, rounding corners.

5 Join Head to top Body seam.

Sitting Dog

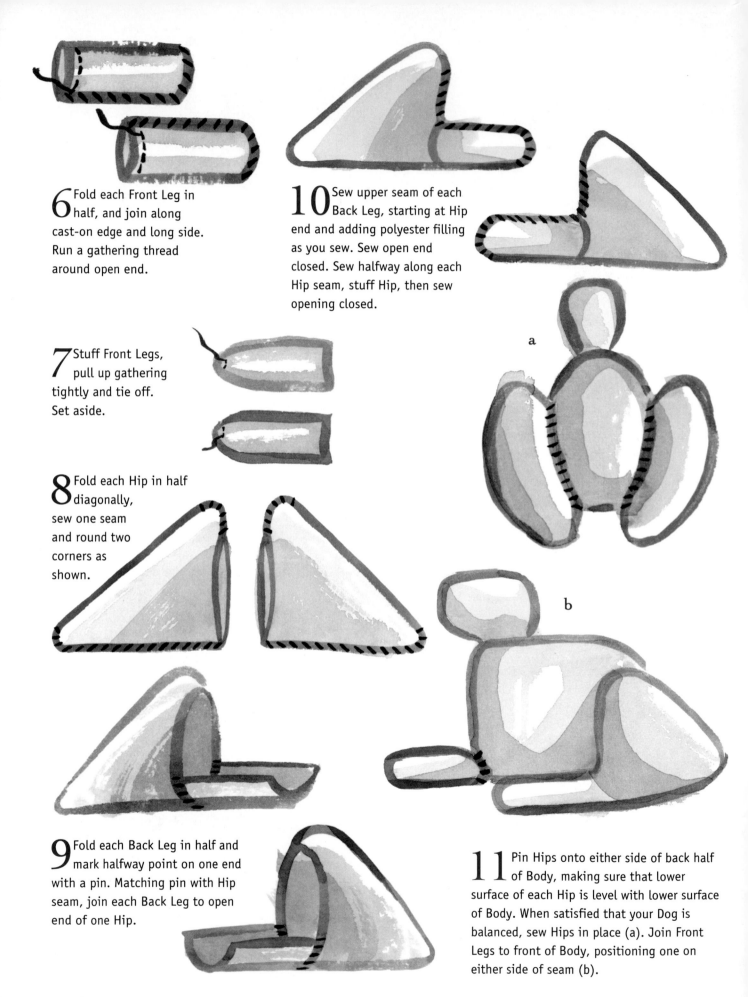

6 Fold each Front Leg in half, and join along cast-on edge and long side. Run a gathering thread around open end.

7 Stuff Front Legs, pull up gathering tightly and tie off. Set aside.

8 Fold each Hip in half diagonally, sew one seam and round two corners as shown.

9 Fold each Back Leg in half and mark halfway point on one end with a pin. Matching pin with Hip seam, join each Back Leg to open end of one Hip.

10 Sew upper seam of each Back Leg, starting at Hip end and adding polyester filling as you sew. Sew open end closed. Sew halfway along each Hip seam, stuff Hip, then sew opening closed.

a

b

11 Pin Hips onto either side of back half of Body, making sure that lower surface of each Hip is level with lower surface of Body. When satisfied that your Dog is balanced, sew Hips in place (a). Join Front Legs to front of Body, positioning one on either side of seam (b).

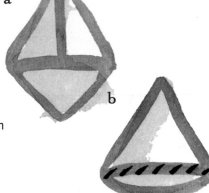

15 Fold each Ear in half diagonally and sew one seam.

16 Arrange each Ear so that seam lies in centre (a), tuck lower corner up inside lower edge and sew along lower edge to close Ear (b).

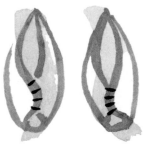

17 With seam at back, fold lower corners across each other and sew in place.

12 Fold Tail piece in half diagonally and sew one seam.

13 Run a gathering thread along seam and gently pull Tail into curved shape. Stuff firmly.

14 Join Tail to top back of Body.

18 Join Ears to top of Head. Using navy, embroider eyes and nose in satin stitch, building up several layers on the nose. Using deep red, embroider mouth in stem stitch. Tie a ribbon around Dog's neck to finish.

Knitting Instructions

Here are instructions for garter stitch, purl stitch, casting on and casting off —
all the knitting techniques you need to know to make the toys in this book.

CASTING ON

Make a loop in the yarn and
insert the left-hand needle (a).
Draw through a loop from the
ball end and tighten the slip
knot (b).

a

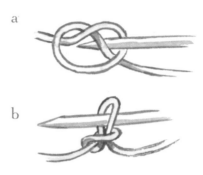

b

Insert the right-hand needle
in the loop and wind the
yarn from the ball around it,
forming a loop.

Pull the loop through and place
it on the left needle. Knit into
it to form the next stitch.

Continue until you have the
required number of stitches
on the left needle.

GARTER, OR KNIT, STITCH

Hold the needle with the
cast-on stitches in your left
hand. With the yarn at the
back of the work, push the
right-hand needle through
the first stitch, from front to
back. Wind the yarn under the
right needle and backwards
over the top, forming a loop.

Pull this loop (the new stitch)
through the first stitch to the
front of the work.

Slip the first stitch off the left
needle, and keep the new
stitch on the right needle.

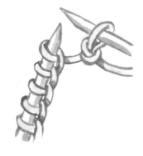

Repeat the above steps until
all stitches have been
transferred to the right needle.

TABLE OF BRITISH EQUIVALENTS

Wool 8-ply = DK

Knitting needles

UK Size	Metric Size (mm)	UK Size	Metric Size (mm)
000	10	7	4.5
00	9	8	4
0	8	9	3.75
1	7.5	–	3.5
2	7	10	3.25
3	6.5	11	3
4	6	12	2.75
5	5.5	13	2.25
6	5	14	2

PURL STITCH

Hold the needle with the cast-on stitches in your left hand. Holding the yarn in front of the work, push the right-hand needle through the first stitch, from back to front. Wind the yarn over and then under the right needle, forming a loop.

Take this loop (the new stitch) through the first stitch to the back of the work.

Slip the first stitch off the left needle, and keep the new stitch on the right needle.

Repeat the above steps until all stitches have been transferred to the right needle.

STOCKING STITCH

To knit stocking stitch, knit one row then purl the next.

CASTING OFF

Knit the first two stitches. * Holding the yarn behind the work, insert the left-hand needle in the first stitch.

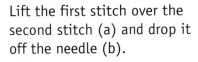

Lift the first stitch over the second stitch (a) and drop it off the needle (b).

a

b

Knit the next stitch * and repeat instructions between the asterisks until one stitch remains on the left-hand needle. Cut the yarn, thread it through the remaining stitch and tighten up gently.

Embroidery Stitches

Work the embroidery on the knitted toys using the following simple stitches:

STRAIGHT STITCH

BUTTONHOLE STITCH

BACKSTITCH

SATIN STITCH

STEM STITCH

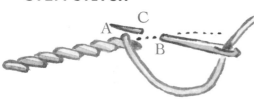

COUCHING STITCH

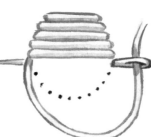

Work from left to right if right-handed. Bring the needle up at A, insert it at B, then bring it back up again at C (the midpoint of the previous stitch), keeping the thread below the needle.